World Rugby

Publisher and Creative Director: Nick Wells
Layout design: Basil
Design and Digital Production: Chris Herbert
Picture Research: Gemma Walters, Rosanna Singler
Senior Editor: Cat Emslie
Copy editor: Bridget Jones
Proofreader: Dawn Laker

Special thanks to: Sam and James at Hayters,
Dave Barends and Ikram Butt

FLAME TREE PUBLISHING

Crabtree Hall, Crabtree Lane
Fulham, London, SW6 6TY
United Kingdom
info@flametreepublishing.com
www.flametreepublishing.com

First published in 2007

07 09 11 10 08
1 3 5 7 9 10 8 6 4 2

Flame Tree is part of The Foundry
Creative Media Company Limited

The CIP record for this book is available from
the British Library.

ISBN 978 1 84451 714 5

Every effort has been made to contact copyright
holders. We apologize in advance for any omissions
and would be pleased to insert the appropriate
acknowledgement in subsequent editions
of this publication.

While every endeavour has been made to ensure
the accuracy of the text and reproduction of the
images in this book, we would be grateful to receive any
comments or suggestions for inclusion in future reprints.

Printed in China

Author and Foreword

MARK RYAN has been a sports journalist for more than
twenty years, and rates the Rugby World Cup Finals of
1991, 1995 and 2003 among the most dramatic events
he has witnessed.

Now in his forties, Ryan's love affair with rugby
stretches back to 1973, when he first began to play the
game as a schoolboy. Facing future British Lions Paul
Thorburn and Rob Ackermann as a teenager showed him
that he would never be good enough to carve out any
kind of career in the game, unless it was through
newspaper reporting. Since then he has worked with
virtually every British national newspaper and written his
first book, *Tie-Break!* which charted the rise of Justine
Henin-Hardenne to the very top of women's tennis.

Also a media trainer, Ryan lives with his wife Victoria
and son Luca in Northamptonshire.

BILL MCLAREN, the 'voice of rugby', was a talented
flanker before tuberculosis forced him to give up playing
the game. However, he went on to become a treasured
commentator for fifty years with the BBC and became
the first non-international to be inducted into the
International Rugby Hall of Fame. His retirement in
2002 marked the end of an era for rugby.

Picture Credits

All photographs courtesy of Empics except:
Corbis: 29, 267, 309, 313, 315; Courtesy of David
Barends: 273; Getty: 7 (cr) & 329, 295; Popperfoto:
269, 277; Shutterstock: 265; Topham Picturepoint: 5 (r)
& 231, 27, 143, 303, 305, 337, 343, 345, 361

World Rugby

Mark Ryan

Foreword: Bill McLaren

**FLAME TREE
PUBLISHING**

Contents

How To Use This Book 8

Foreword 10

Introduction 12

Union v League 14

Oceania 16

1900s Dave Gallaher's 'Originals' *to* 'Dally' Messenger 18–23

1920s George Nepia *to* 'Johnny' Wallace and Waratahs 24–27

1930s The Bledisloe Cup *to* Fiji in New Zealand 28–31

1950s Australia 25 New Zealnd 49 *to* Colin Meads 32–43

1960s Ken Catchpole *to* Ian Kirkpatrick 44–51

1970s Greg Cornelsen *to* Graham Mourie's Grand Slam Dramatists 52–61

1980s The Flour-Bomb Test *to* Tim Horan.......................................62–85

1990s 'Willy' Ofahengaue *to* Christian Cullen 86–111

2000s Australia Beat British Lions *to* Dan Carter 112–129

Europe 130

1800s William Webb Ellis *to* Beginnings of Rugby League 132–137

1910s England's First Back-to-Back Grand Slams 138–139

1920s Wavell Wakefield 140–141

1930s Jean Galia *to* Gus Risman...................................142–147

1940s Jackie Kyle *to* Brian Bevan 148–153

1950s Dave Valentine *to* Tony O'Reilly 154–163

1960s David Duckham *to* France's First Grand Slam...................164–169

1970s Great Britain Win Ashes Down Under *to* Bill Beaumont 170–191

1980s The Rise of the Oaks *to* Serge Blanco 192–197

1990s Ellery Hanley *to* France Beat All Blacks 15-31 198–217

2000s Italy Win Six Nations Opener *to* The Rise of Georgia..........218–243

Africa **244**

1900s The Green Jersey Adopted *to* Tour of Britain......................246–249

1920s Springboks First Tour of New Zealand 250–251

1930s Danie Craven, Player and Coach 252–253

1950s Hennie Muller *to* False Start of Rugby League 254–259

1960s Frik du Preez *to* Death Knell for Rugby League 260–265

1970s Anti-Apartheid Demonstrations *to* David Barends 266–271

1980s Naas Botha *to* Zimbabwe Play in the First World Cup 272–277

1990s Namibia Beat Ireland and Italy *to* Joost van der Westhuizen ..278–293

2000s Rhinos Lose to France *to* Percy Montgomery 294–297

Americas **298**

1800s First Recorded Rugby Match on American Soil 300–301

1910s Argentina 3 Combined Britain 28 302–303

1920s USA Win Olympic Rugby Gold 304–305

1960s The Pumas are Born...306–307

1970s Old Christians of Uruguay Forced to Eat Human Flesh 308–309

1980s Jaguars Beat The Springboks *to* Canada Beat USA 310–319

1990s Canada Reach Quarter Finals *to* Canada Beat Wales 320–327

2000s Argentina 152 Paraguay 0 *to* Positive Outlook for Pumas ..328–339

Asia **340**

1800s Rugby first introduced to Japan 342–343

1920s Japan Rugby Football Union Formed 344–345

1970s Japan 3 England 6 *to* First Hong Kong Sevens 346–349

1980s Toshiyuki Hayashi *to* Japan 28 Scotland 24 350–355

1990s Hong Kong Sevens' Heroes *to* Andrew McCormick 356–367

2000s Lebanon Beat France 36-6 *to* Daisuke Ohata 368–379

Index 380

How To Use This Book

You are encouraged to use this book in a variety of ways, each of which caters for a range of interests, knowledge and uses.

- The book is organized by the main geographical areas in which rugby is played, and within those chapters it is chronological. In *general*, where more than one area is relevant, the entry is placed within the region that gained a positive result or for which the entry is most significant.
- The entries relate to all aspects of the game: players, teams, managers, matches and events – triumphs, defeats, tragedies, landmarks.
- The geographical and chronological format provides the reader with a fascinating journey through time and space, to discover less well-known players, teams and topics alongside the familiar ones.
- The comprehensive index enables the reader to find specific names quickly and easily.

David Campese

Campo

1980s–90s David Campese is regarded as one of the greatest flank players of all time. He played a major part in his country's Rugby World Cup triumph of 1991. Not only did his famous goose step often wrongfoot mesmerized opponents, but also, his taste for psychological warfare meant that rival teams were sometimes half-beaten before a match had even begun.

A maverick, Campese was also prone to the occasional catastrophic error, such as the one that cost Australia the 1989 Test Series against the British Lions. He lived on the edge and had his attempted interception in the dying minutes of the 1991 World Cup final against England been ruled a deliberate knock-on, Australia might not have gone home with the William Webb Ellis trophy.

Campese's place in history was always assured, whatever the achievements of the teams he played for. His final total of 46 international tries was a world record, beaten in only 2006. He is best remembered for the outrageous talent he oozed from every pore, his power and blistering pace and, above all, the wonderful unpredictability that helped him to become one of the greatest entertainers the rugby world has ever seen. Campese in full flight, leaving opponents for dead as he roared towards the try-line, remains one of the sport's most enduring and beautiful sights.

David Campese
Born 21 October 1962
Place of birth Queanbeyan, Australia
Caps 101
Teams Australia

2. Subtitle gives extra information about the subject of the entry.

1. Entry title

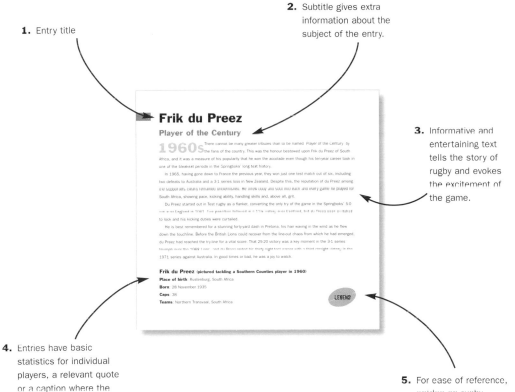

Frik du Preez
Player of the Century

1960s There cannot be many greater tributes than to be named 'Player of the Century' by the fans of the country. This was the honour bestowed upon Frik du Preez of South Africa, and it was a measure of his popularity that he won the accolade even though his ten-year career took in one of the bleakest periods in the Springboks' long test history.

In 1965, having gone down to France the previous year, they won just one test match out of six, including two defeats to Australia and a 3-1 series loss in New Zealand. Despite this, the reputation of du Preez among the supporters clearly remained unblemished. He threw body and soul into each and every game he played for South Africa, showing pace, kicking ability, handling skills and, above all, grit.

Du Preez started out in Test rugby as a flanker, converting the only try of the game in the Springboks' 5-0 win over England in 1961. Two positions followed in a 7/9 victory over Scotland, but du Preez soon switched to lock and his kicking duties were curtailed.

He is best remembered for a stunning forty-yard dash in Pretoria, his hair waving in the wind as he flew down the touchline. Before the British Lions could recover from the line-out chaos from which he had emerged, du Preez had reached the try-line for a vital score. That 25-20 victory was a key moment in the 3-1 series triumph over the 1968 Lions, and du Preez ended his thirty-eight test career with a third straight victory in the 1971 series against Australia. In good times or bad, he was a joy to watch.

Frik du Preez (pictured tackling a Southern Counties player in 1960)
Place of birth: Rustenburg, South Africa
Born: 28 November 1935
Caps: 38
Teams: Northern Transvaal, South Africa

LEGEND

3. Informative and entertaining text tells the story of rugby and evokes the excitement of the game.

4. Entries have basic statistics for individual players, a relevant quote or a caption where the picture needs explaining.

5. For ease of reference, entries on rugby legends or memorable landmarks in the sport are highlighted by these icons, colour coded by chapter.

Foreword

Rugby is a game that has brought me enormous pleasure through the course of my life and work. From the bravery and skill of the players to the passion and enthusiasm of the supporters, even after over fifty years of commentating on the sport, rugby never ceases to inspire.

I am delighted to put my name to this book, which gives an in-depth look at the game across the world, even including notables from rugby league. It is truly wide-ranging, giving a real feel of how the game has developed and prospered.

Whether you read it cover to cover or dip in and out to savour your favourite moments, there is so much to rejoice in. Key moments from rugby's roots in the nineteenth century are brought to life right up until how the game is played today. The legendary players and characters, the many tournaments, classic triumphs and defeats and even events revealing rugby's importance in the wider world of politics are all covered. Of course you can't please everyone – but I know my personal favourite is that great day in 1990 when Scotland defeated England to win the Grand Slam. I can still hear the crowd's roar ringing in my ears!

From Murrayfield to Dunedin, the values of respect and enjoyment endure. This book encapsulates that spirit. Enjoy!

Introduction

This book is for rugby lovers, pure and simple. While more space is devoted to rugby union, it seemed wrong to ignore some of rugby league's most dazzling stars and moments, particularly as so many players have crossed from one code to the other. Who can forget that it was Jason Robinson, a former rugby league ace, who scored England's only try in rugby union's World Cup final of 2003?

After more than a century of tension between league and union, it is, perhaps, time for a few more barriers to come down. It is easy to forget that supporters of each code appreciate similar qualities in their heroes: hard men; pin-point kickers; and, above all, athletic, powerful speed merchants – men who convey the sheer thrill of running with the ball.

This compact collection has been compiled with such a spirit of rugby in mind and there are plenty of memories for fans of both codes to enjoy, especially if spectacular, exceptional moments and people are what remain fascinating. There simply is not sufficient space to include everything and everyone; if omissions spark fierce debate about rugby's all-time greats, so much the better. Please accept my apologies for any offence caused and remember that differing opinions are also very much a part of our enjoyment of sport. Researching the material has been something of a rollercoaster ride, not just a journey around the globe, but through time itself. If even a part of that exhilaration is conveyed to the reader, then the objective will have been achieved.

The pictures and words tell the story, without pretension or prejudice, of how the game of rugby was born and exported to far-flung corners of the earth, and illustrate why code-hopping is by no means just a modern phenomenon. The incredible success of rugby union's World Cup, even before the game turned professional in 1995, has surprised many observers. Continents are now coming together as never before to celebrate their love of the game and match their individual strengths and weaknesses against rival playing styles. At this level, perhaps, though played worldwide, rugby league still has some catching up to do.

Considering such dramatic growth, this book has been split into separate sections on Oceania, Europe, Africa, the Americas, and Asia. It may be no coincidence that Oceania, where rugby's rival codes are played with a common emphasis on raw running power, has produced the most consistently successful teams in either game – Australia and New Zealand. New Zealand, in particular, went into 2007 having taken rugby union to a new level, with their swift passing game and devastating flare on the counter-attack.

And so to the other side of the world and Europe, with its mix of countries and rugby union styles. Often criticized for the stiff predictability of their rugby, nonetheless England entered 2007 as World Cup holders. By recruiting key figures from rugby league, such as Jason Robinson and Phil Larder (the coach appointed as 'Advisor on Defence'), their gain was plain for all to see. The explosive power and solid defence that characterized England's 2003 World Cup campaign seemed to owe a great deal to the cornerstones on which rugby league was built.

For sheer passion, South Africa's love of rugby is unsurpassed worldwide, even though it doesn't tell Africa's whole story. Anyone underestimating the resilience of the game in the Americas would have been shocked in late 2006, when Argentina came to Twickenham and humbled the sport's inventors for the very first time on their revered turf. Asia has long played host to rugby union's best-loved party, the Hong Kong Sevens, and Japan is now leading the way on the rest of the continent's relatively untapped stage.

Oceania's fans in particular knew that whatever happened next, the spell-binding drama of world rugby would continue to offer unforgettable moments and characters. It always has, and always will.

Mark Ryan

Union v League

A Healthy Rivalry

In 1895 a breakaway movement turned its back on rugby union and set up a professional sport called rugby league. One hundred years later, rugby union followed the rival code's example when it also turned professional.

Now, in the twenty-first century, it could be argued that the respective games have never been closer. These days, as has long been the case in league, it is necessary for all top union players to be powerful runners, strong tacklers and good ball handlers. Fundamental differences remain: there are no line-outs in rugby league, no flankers in the thirteen-man game, and certainly no rucks or mauls; scrums are uncontested. At the time of writing, there is an on-going debate within rugby union over whether their scrums should become uncontested due to the number of serious spinal injuries sustained among collapsed front rows.

It would be wrong to suggest that rugby union is becoming rugby league, even though union has recruited some of the rival code's top players and coaches. It is hard to imagine, for example, a day when union players heel the ball back through their legs when tackled. However, union fans no longer look down on rugby league as they once did. Instead, they respect the strength and athleticism of the game from which some of their favourites have come.

The codes may never reunite, but there now seem to be fewer reasons to prolong the tensions and prejudices of the past. At long last we can focus on the common beauty of both games, epitomized by the sheer joy of running with the ball.

Opposite: Australia's George Gregan (left) flies with the ball during Rugby *Union's* 2006 Tri-Nations, while Kiwi Stacey Jones (right), International Rugby League Player of the Year, evades a tackle in Rugby *League's* 2006 Tri-Nations.

OCEANIA

If rugby lovers had to pick a corner of the earth where the game is played exactly as it should be – with thrills guaranteed – few would look further than Oceania.

In rugby union, Australia won the World Cup twice in the twentieth century, a fitting reward for their adventure and bravery. David Campese typified the expansive Wallaby spirit, as did Dally Messenger in the early days of rugby league. When it comes to flare players, Australia's neighbours often seem to have more than will fit into any single team. From Dave Gallaher to Dan Carter, the awesome All Blacks have been feared and admired in equal measure.

New Zealand and Australia continue to set the standard for world rugby, dominating both codes. Throw in the breathtaking rugby union magic of Fiji, add the raw aggression of Pacific islanders, Western Samoa and Tonga, and you have a very special rugby paradise. Oceania is, quite simply, the envy of the world.

Dave Gallaher's Originals

The First All Blacks

1900s Dave Gallaher, a feisty wing forward, wrote his name into New Zealand rugby history when he led his country's finest players on a highly successful tour of Britain and France in 1905–06. It was the first time they were described as the All Blacks, a reference to their simple playing strip that soon started to strike fear into opponents. Gallaher's tourists also became known as The Originals, and set the standard for the awesome All Black sides of the future.

They won four out of five internationals, losing only to Wales, 0-3, under controversial circumstances. In Cardiff, New Zealand were disallowed what they thought was a perfectly good try. Away from the test arena, they won the other twenty matches so easily that they rarely conceded a point.

Interestingly, the diplomacy did not always match the dominance on the field, a culture clash that was also a sign of things to come for the All Blacks' tours. Gallaher's brand of rugby was regarded as unnecessarily brutal by some British and he complained, 'I must confess that the unfair criticism to which I have been subjected, while in Wales especially, has annoyed me'.

He died at Passchendale aged 43, having volunteered for the First World War.

Dave Gallaher

Born: 30 October 1873   **Died**: 4 October 1917
Place of birth: Ramelton, Ireland
Caps: 6
Teams: New Zealand

'Dally' Messenger

Innovative and Brilliant

1900s Herbert Henry 'Dally' Messenger was one of Australia's earliest rugby entertainers, a maverick who might even have put David Campese in the shade had they ever played together. He represented Australia twice at rugby union, switched to rugby league and New Zealand for three tests, then played the same code seven times for Australia. Such was Messenger's innovative brilliance that he even kept the rule-makers busy as they sought to stay apace with his ideas. His impact on the game was so great that Australian rugby league's Player of the Year is awarded a 'Dally M. Medal' to this day.

An elusive and highly tricky centre, Messenger was expelled from rugby union after accepting money to play two tests for Australia against a professional New Zealand team in 1907. He reacted by joining the New Zealanders on a tour to Britain, where he was the outstanding player as they adopted rugby league rules. Returning to Australia, Dally quickly became a crowd-pleasing superstar and captained his country in three tests. During his colourful career he is reported to have kicked a field goal while held around one leg, punched the ball over the opposition before catching it to score, and trampled all over a collapsed scrum on his way to the try-line. Messenger was, quite simply, a one-off.

'Dally' Messenger

Born: 12 April 1883   **Died**: 24 November 1959

Place of birth: Balmain, Australia

Caps: 2

Teams: Eastern Suburbs, New South Wales, Australia, New Zealand

Opposite: Dally Messenger having a beer with two friends under a photograph of himself in his playing days.

SYDNEY FLYING SQUADRON

THE MASTER

George Nepia

With The Invincibles

1920s George Nepia was still a teenager when he was picked to tour Britain in 1924. As a Maori, he was particularly proud to lead his team-mates in a version of the Haka said to have been composed especially for the tour. Although the New Zealand Maoris had first brought the much-loved war-dance to rugby in the latter part of the previous century, it is Nepia and the 1924 tourists who are credited with introducing the Haka on the biggest sporting stage.

Opponents would have done well to heed the Haka's warning. The nineteen-year-old's fierce tackling and astute kicking helped the All Blacks remain unbeaten that year in Britain, and the team quickly became known as The Invincibles.

Nepia played in all thirty-two matches, amassing seventy-seven points along the way. He went on to play thirty-eight consecutive games for his country, a record. Therefore, his omission from the 1928 tour to South Africa, probably for no other reason than the colour of his skin, was particularly conspicuous.

In 1935 Nepia returned to England to play rugby league professionally and represented his country in that code too. Later he returned to union and played a first class match against his son, also called George, at the ripe old age of forty-five.

George Nepia

Born: 25 April 1905   **Died**: 27 August 1986
Place of birth: Wairoa, New Zealand
Caps: 10
Teams: Hawkes Bay, New Zealand, New Zealand Maori

LEGEND

Barefoot Warriors

Tonga's Tour to Fiji

1926 The arrival of Tonga for their first tour to Fiji in 1926 was also the first time their hosts adopted their famous white jerseys with palm-tree badge and black shorts.

Fiji won the opening test of the three to be played at Albert Park, Suva, 10-3; but Tonga hit back in the second match with a gutsy 13-8 victory. When it came to the deciding encounter, witnessed by a touring college team from Auckland, everything rested on an unknown Tongan penalty-kicker wearing nothing on his feet. With the pressure on, he carved out a hole on the half-way line with his bare heel, something the New Zealand boys found almost impossible to do in the hard ground when they tried later wearing boots. The spectators all watched in awe as a mighty thud of exposed toes on unforgiving leather signalled the launch on a flight path that took the ball half the length of the pitch and straight between the posts for a dramatic, and series-deciding, 6-3 victory.

Such a reverse on their own soil would have been hard for the Fijians to take. When they toured Tonga two years later, one of the test matches had to be abandoned due to fighting.

Opposite: Tongan rugby today. The Tongans always start their matches with a war dance – the Kailao. The dance is traditionally used to display the dancers' discipline, obedience and skill with their weapon, although on the rugby pitch, the players perform the dance without their weapons!

'Johnny' Wallace and Waratahs

Inventors of Adventurous Running Rugby

1927–28 The New South Wales Waratahs are credited with inventing the open, adventurous style that has been the hallmark of Australian rugby ever since. Their running rugby evolved on a landmark tour of Britain, France and Canada between 1927 and 1928. To the astonishment of spectators, the Australian side averaged almost four tries per game in the thirty-one matches they played. Captained by 'Johnny' Wallace (who had played nine times for Scotland), the Australians won twenty-four and drew two of those fixtures, beating Ireland, Wales and France at international level. Their high-risk rugby might have cost them against the experience of Scotland and England, who both beat the Waratahs, but it was that emphasis they placed on running rugby, with forwards and backs sweeping downfield together, that captured the imagination. Perhaps that was why they were treated to a parade through Sydney and a reception at the town hall when they finally got home.

Wallace and the Waratahs were never forgotten, though it was not until 1986 that the landmark games against the Five Nations were given retrospective international status. That belated honour would have tickled Wallace, who died in 1975. As a Scottish international, he had scored a crucial try to help beat England at Murrayfield in 1925. Now, long after his death, he was an Aussie international too.

Opposite: Riding high on their success the Waratahs are received by King George V at Sandringham, 4 February 1928.

The Magic Begins

The Bledisloe Cup

1931 Not even Lord Bledisloe, Governor-General of New Zealand, could have known quite what he was starting when he donated the Bledisloe Cup back in 1931. Three-quarters of a century of high-intensity conflict has followed, and the arguments have not been confined to the pitch. For example, the Australian Rugby Union reckons the trophy was first fought for that same year, when the All Blacks beat their rivals 20-13 in Auckland. New Zealanders, meanwhile, maintain that they only began to play for the trophy on tour to Australia in 1932.

Whoever is right, it was not until 1934 that Australia first won the cup, and that early pattern continued over the years. At the start of the twenty-first century, the All Blacks had won the Bledisloe Cup about three times as often as the Australians; however, the turn of the century saw Australia register the biggest Bledisloe Cup crowd of all time, an incredible 109,874 at Stadium Australia.

It is a compliment to Lord Bledisloe's generosity all those years ago that the world's two best teams have never tired of knocking lumps out of each other in order to get their hands on his handsome cup.

'The Bledisloe Cup is a huge trophy for New Zealand rugby. New Zealanders are very proud of it, as are the team. It's probably the major trophy that we play for, apart from the one we play for every four years [the World Cup].'

New Zealand coach Graham Henry

Achieving The Impossible

Fiji in New Zealand

1939 In this memorable year, Fiji achieved the near-impossible in rugby terms – they toured New Zealand and came away unbeaten. The fact that it was also the Fijians' first tour of the rugby-mad country makes the aura surrounding their invincibility that year all the more enduring.

Knowing the importance of raw, warrior-like aggression if they were to stand a chance on the tour, Fiji's captain, the magnificently named Ratu Sir George Cakobau realized that his team needed a weapon with which to neutralize the fearsome Maori Haka. So he consulted Ratu Bola, chief of the Navusaradave warriors in Bau, who offered to teach Fiji's rugby players a routine of their own.

In this way, the 'Cibi' was unleashed on the rugby world and this war dance has remained Fiji's challenge to opposing teams ever since. It certainly worked its magic on that historic tour of 1939, when New Zealand sides were staggered to find themselves overrun by a team dominated by runners still playing barefoot rugby.

Those who were not so shocked, such as the Maoris, generally lost anyway. Fiji won seven and drew one on that tour, beating the Maoris 14-4 along the way. No other team has ever left New Zealand with quite such an impressive record, not even those who have taken on the world's most daunting challenge in boots.

Opposite: Fiji still rely on the imposing and forceful
Cibi to challenge their opponents. Here Bill Cavubati
leads the Fijian war dance at North Harbour Stadium in
New Zealand, 2005.

Record-Breakers (LEAGUE)

Australia 25 New Zealand 49

1952 Desmond White, the New Zealand full-back from Auckland, kicked his way into the rugby league record books in front of 30,000 stunned spectators at the Gabba Ground in Brisbane on 28 June 1952. He landed an incredible eleven goals in the second test against Australia, helping his side to an astonishing 49-25 victory. Not surprisingly, White's 'Eleven from Heaven' were a world record. For Australia, the reverse offered nothing but unwanted records. It was their greatest margin of defeat in a test match, and the most points they had ever conceded. Ironically, the margin could have been much worse, because the Kiwis were 42-10 ahead until three late Aussie tries salvaged just a hint of pride.

White could not take all the credit though. Rampant three-quarters Tom Baxter and Cyril Eastlake showed why they were rated among the best in the world, while half-backs George Menzies and former All Black Jim Haig were at the sharp end of the destruction. George Crawford of the *Daily Telegraph* wrote, 'Even the selectors laughed at the efforts of the Australians to check the New Zealand advance'. The Kiwis took the series to complete the humiliation.

Opposite: Over 50 years after Desmond White's triumph, New Zealand continues to court success as players celebrate another victory over Australia, having beaten them in the Rugby League Tri-Nations final at Elland Road, Leeds, England, on 26 November 2005.

Solomon's Minders

South Africa 14 Australia 18

1953 Imagine doing something so remarkable in sport that you are chaired off the field in triumph – by members of the opposing team. It happened to the Wallabies' captain, John Solomon, in 1953. His team had just defeated South Africa at Newlands, Cape Town, in the shadow of the mighty Table Mountain.

The Wallabies had not clinched the series, in fact they ended up losing it 3-1. What made that 18-14 victory in the second test so special was the knowledge that the all-conquering Springboks had not lost for fifteen years.

With extraordinary sportsmanship, given that their team's amazing run had just come to a painful end, the South African crowd gave the Australians a standing ovation. The host nation's players were even more generous: in recognition of a deserved victory, they lifted Solomon on to their shoulders and carried him off the field to loud cheers, leaving the rest of the victorious Australian team dumbfounded. Hardened characters such as Cyril Burke, 'Spanner' Brown, Mac Hughes, Col Windon and Bob Outside were left wondering if they could trust their eyes or believe what they had done.

Opposite: Table Mountain looms in the background during a match at Newlands stadium in 1953.

On Top of The World (LEAGUE)

Australia Win the 1957 World Cup

1957 Having lost to Great Britain only seven months earlier in England, it seemed a tall order for Australia to win the second World Cup, even in their own country. The fact that the 1957 World Cup marked the fiftieth anniversary of rugby league in their country would only have added to the sense of expectation. However, Australian captain, Dick Poole, began to sense that new confidence was flowing into his side when they beat New Zealand 25-5 in Brisbane. That comfortable win not only put their campaign in motion, but also set up an enthralling showdown with the British in front of 57,955 fans at the Sydney Cricket Ground. However, they had picked up injuries in that first victory, and few expected makeshift full-back Brian Carlson or stand-in scrum-half Ken McCaffery to be quite as devastating against the favourites. They ran riot as the Aussies triumphed 31-6 and future captain Carlson was to end with the individual award for Australia's best player in the tournament.

Since a league format was being used, Poole's surprise packages now knew they had only to beat France in order to claim the title. They did so with typical fluency, winning 29-9, and the trophy was theirs before the matches were even completed. Soon after being crowned world champions, they proved it was no fluke by defeating a Rest of the World side in Sydney 20-11. Now no one could argue. The men from Down Under really were tops.

Opposite: The fateful game which Australia lost to Great Britain in the year before they turned it all around and won the World Cup.

Don Clarke

The Boot

1950s–60s

Don Clarke became the perfect rugby union full-back but as a teenager it looked as though he could turn his hand to any sporting role he chose. At the tender age of seventeen he opened the bowling for Auckland, though he was also playing rugby for the highly respected Waikato. His six-feet-two-inch frame gave him the perfect physique for either game, and he enjoyed both. However, something had to give sooner or later and in New Zealand, where rugby is almost a religion, it was not hard for Clarke to choose to pursue the number one sport. His amazing talent for goal-kicking set the records tumbling during a test career that spanned from 1956 to 1964, and earned him a simple nickname – The Boot. In eighty-nine matches for the All Blacks, including thirty-one tests, he struck an extraordinary 781 points. It was a record that stood proudly for twenty-four years, until another All Black legend, Grant Fox, finally passed Clarke's total in 1988.

One of The Boot's best moments came in his very first year in the cauldron of international rugby. The pressure of the big-time stage did not seem to bother him at all, and he kicked the decisive penalties to land New Zealand their first ever series win against the Springboks.

He was not simply a goal-kicker. Clarke rarely missed a tackle and he really was Mr Reliable in the international arena. In 1961 he made history at a lower level when he turned out for a Waikato team also featuring all four of his brothers – Ian, Doug, Brian and Graeme. By then he was already well on his way to becoming an All Black all-time-great.

Don Clarke

Born: 10 November 1933   **Died**: 29 December 2002

Place of birth: Pihama, New Zealand

Caps: 31

Teams: New Zealand

Wilson Whineray

Leader From The Front

1950s–60s A fearsome prop, Wilson Whineray captained the All Blacks in thirty tests, a remarkable achievement during the 1950s and 60s, when far fewer internationals were played. The fact that he spearheaded victories in twenty-three of those matches (losing only four), highlighted how inspirational he was as skipper.

He was only twenty-three when he captained the All Blacks against the Wallabies in 1958 and led from the front by charging over for two tries. His toughest opponent was Pier du Toit, who gave him a rough ride on the tour to South Africa in 1960. Many believe he used such experiences to his advantage and got even better with age.

Certainly, no one could match his confidence and power on the 1963–64 tour of Britain and France. One of the most memorable moments of his distinguished career came against the Barbarians in 1964. Acting more like a stand-off than a tight-head, Whineray threw an outrageous dummy and left the Barbarian defence for dead as he raced clear to score. He was not always so frivolous, however, and a failure to connect with younger All Blacks may have contributed to the closure of his test career at the age of thirty.

In total, he played for New Zealand seventy-seven times, and was even known to stitch from the front to the back row when necessary. He played in thirty-two internationals between 1957 and 1965, and retired with a reputation as a natural born winner.

Wilson Whineray

Born: 10 July 1935
Place of birth: Auckland, New Zealand
Caps: 32
Teams: New Zealand

Colin Meads

Pinetree

1950s–70s A legendary hard man with the build to match, Colin Meads battled for the All Blacks in 133 matches during a career that spanned three decades. He was the first New Zealand player to reach a half-century of test caps, starting in 1957 and finishing on fifty-five in 1971.

In the modern era, with its more crowded international schedule, there is little doubt that Meads would have reached the one-hundred-cap milestone. The farmer from King Country earned his nickname, Pinetree, because he was six feet three inches tall and as durable as they come. He was not slow to use his power and ruthlessly punished any opposing players who dared to infringe or stray offside. Not only did Meads tour Australia with the All Blacks aged just twenty-one, but he also played in both tests and even scored a try when he was switched from flanker out to the wing due to an injury.

He went on to score six more tries for his country, and was feared around the world in his familiar position in the second row. Perhaps his most memorable score was to clinch the second test win in South Africa in 1960. An awesome force on the 1963-64 tour of Britain and France, he also inspired series wins against the Springboks and Lions from 1965-66. Another highly successful tour of Britain in 1967 demonstrated his consistency.

Time caught up with him in the end. Aged 34, he broke an arm vice-captaining his country in South Africa in 1970 and by the time he actually skippered the All Blacks in the memorable 1971 series against the British Lions, he had already seen better, bruising days.

Colin Meads

Born: 3 June 1936
Place of birth: Cambridge, New Zealand
Caps: 56
Teams: New Zealand

LEGEND

Ken Catchpole

The Greatest

1960s Even during his relatively short career, Ken Catchpole was described as 'the greatest half-back the world has ever known'. The accolade came from the president of England's RFU after Catchpole had led Australia to victory at Twickenham on the tour of 1967–68. Wales also fell victim to Catchpole's genius that winter, when the unplayable scrum-half simply ran riot.

Aged just twenty-one, Catchpole had made his international debut as captain, one of only nine players ever to begin a test career with such responsibility on their shoulders. It did not seem to bother him, and Fiji were comprehensively beaten in that three-match series of 1961. As Catchpole's partnership with Phil Hawthorne became almost telepathic at half-back, Australia's success story extended to new chapters. The Wallabies won both tests against South Africa in 1965, a highlight of the Catchpole era.

It was something of a tragedy for rugby that the little genius had his career cut short in 1968, when he was unceremoniously removed from a ruck by the fearsome All Black forward, Colin Meads. Catchpole was forced to retire at the age of twenty-nine. He had played twenty-seven test matches, thirteen as captain, but the sport was robbed of the climax his talent deserved.

Ken Catchpole

Born: 21 June 1939
Place of birth: Paddington, Australia
Caps: 27
Teams: New South Wales, Australia

Reg Gasnier (LEAGUE)

Puff the Magic Dragon

1960s This 'Prince of Centres' had no equal during a scintillating career in the late fifties and sixties. He either scored or created many of the best tries of his era, bursting through classy defences with head back and legs pumping all the way to the try-line. He was known as Puff the Magic Dragon, not only because he played for St George Dragons, but also because his unique change of pace meant he could disappear in the blink of an eye.

If he found a way through the opposition once, more often than not he would go on to rip them to shreds. Gasnier scored three tries for New South Wales on his debut aged eighteen, and repeated the feat in his second test appearance in 1959 against the touring Kiwis.

There was yet another hat-trick against the British on the Kangaroos' 1959-60 tour, during a 22-14 test win at Widnes. Gasnier finished a series loser though, as he did against the British Lions after being made Australia's youngest captain at twenty-three years and twenty-eight days.

He would have spectacular revenge, warming up with successful home-series wins against South Africa and New Zealand in 1963. Then it was back to Britain with the Kangaroos, and this time the hosts were humiliated. Gasnier scored two tries in the 28-2 first test win at Wembley, then teamed up with fellow centre Graeme Langlands to lead what became known as the 'Swinton Massacre'. By the time Gasnier stopped swerving and sprinting, Australia had put 50 points on the board to win the Ashes.

One of the world's greatest ever rugby runners, Gasnier retired, aged just twenty-eight, with a cruciate injury.

Reg Gasnier

Born: 1939
Place of birth: Kogarah, New South Wales
Caps: 36
Teams: St George Dragons, Australia

Johnny Raper (LEAGUE)

Lock with Smoking Barrels

1960s Hailed as the best lock-forward the world of rugby league had ever seen, Johnny Raper handled like a dream and tackled so ferociously that he became every opponent's nightmare. Raper was not merely a part of the Kangaroos' greatest moments in the 1960s, he created many of them.

Although he scored a try on his test debut at Wigan in 1959, he could not prevent defeat to the British on that particular occasion. However, revenge was especially sweet on his return to northern England in 1963, when he played a leading role in the first touring Australian team to win the Ashes in fifty years of trying.

In the second test at Swinton, Raper not only had a hand in the seven tries the Aussies nailed on their stunned hosts in the first twenty-five minutes, but he actually gave the scoring pass in four of them.

Swinton became the happiest of hunting grounds again on the 1967–68 Ashes tour, as Raper recovered from a fractured cheekbone in time to captain his country to glory in the 11-3 third test decider. He also led Australia to World Cup triumph in 1968, as they confirmed their supremacy with a comfortable 20-2 win over France in the final in front of their own fans at the Sydney Cricket Ground.

Johnny Raper (Opposite: back row, 4th from left)

Born: 12 April 1939

Place of birth: Sydney, Australia

Caps: 33

Teams: Newtown Jets, St George Dragons, New South Wales, Australia

Ian Kirkpatrick

The Flanker Who Could Not Stop Scoring

1960s–70s A blind-side specialist before the role was fully understood, Ian Kirkpatrick wrote his name into All Black folklore relatively early in his distinguished international career.

Any player who sits on the substitutes' bench is faced with a formidable psychological challenge. He must keep the adrenalin flowing, even if deep down he suspects it will never be used. In 1968, Kirkpatrick stayed mentally and physically sharp on the sidelines, as favoured squad-mates did battle against Australia in Sydney. When his turn came, he answered the call heroically. By the time the final whistle blew, he had shown just what a devastating weapon he could be, scoring an historic hat-trick of tries to secure his place in rugby legend.

An amazing 115 tries in 289 first class matches showed that his Sydney heroics were no one-off. Few forwards ever reach the seemingly untouchable century milestone, but Kirkpatrick just kept on going.

He captained the All Blacks nine times in thirty-eight tests, scoring 16 international tries before being replaced at the helm without warning in 1974. Not even the greats are always well-treated when selectors decide it is time for them to make way.

Ian Kirkpatrick

Born: 24 May 1946
Place of birth: Gisborne, New Zealand
Caps: 39
Teams: New Zealand

Greg Cornelsen

Four-Try Legend

1970s Rarely will a sporting legend be defined by one moment in his international career. It was not that Greg Cornelsen ever appeared anything but competent on the twenty-five occasions he represented his country. Only nine of those matches were won, but the flanker never let his country down. However, Cornelsen shot from journeyman to legend in 1978, when the Wallabies faced New Zealand at Eden Park, having already lost a three-match series against their deadliest rivals and facing the humiliation of a 'Blackwash'. Were the All Blacks lacking their customary cutting edge, having already won the first two tests? Maybe, but Cornelsen certainly punished any complacency in dramatic style to salvage Australia's pride.

Running in no fewer than four tries, he cut the famed home defence to ribbons as the Wallabies went home 30-16 victors in the only match of the three that will be remembered for ever. No player has ever scored so many tries in a test match between the world's two finest rugby nations.

Greg Cornelsen

Born: 29 August 1952

Place of birth: Sydney, Australia

Caps: 25

Teams: Australia

A Very Difficult Afternoon

Fiji Humble The Barbarians 29-9

1970 When some of rugby's biggest names agreed to play unknown quantities Fiji, in the north-eastern rugby outpost of Gosforth, England, they did not anticipate a very difficult afternoon. In 1970 there was no brighter star than Gareth Edwards of Wales and he travelled to the match in relaxed mood, ready to teach the Pacific islanders a rugby lesson. His confidence, as he soon discovered, was somewhat misplaced.

Remembering the occasion to this day, Edwards recently recalled, 'It was supposed to be a bit of an exhibition game, with the likes of Phil Bennett, David Duckham and Derek Quinell in a strong Baa-Baas side, but we completely underestimated the Fijians, and instead of strutting our stuff, we spent eighty minutes chasing shadows.'

Fiji ran in seven crushing tries as they simply ran riot. Their winger, Asaeli Batibasaga, bagged one try and landed four conversions. Back row star Ilaitia Tuisese also dived over during the mayhem. Edwards watched astonished as Senitike Nasave, Josaia Visei, Antonio Racika, Jo Qoro and Nasivi Ravouvou joined in the romp and left world-renowned players looking like hopeless novices. Only Duckham and John Spencer scored ties for the Barbarians.

Edwards admitted later, 'It was a game that tarnished a number of reputations and even cost one or two players their places on the 1971 tour to New Zealand.' It was also one of Fiji's finest hours.

Opposite: Gareth Edwards playing for Wales in a more successful game, feeding his backs in the Five Nations Championship in 1970 where his team won 18-9 to Scotland.

The Woeful Wallabies

Tonga Beat Australia 16-11

1973 On 30 June 1973, in Ballymore, Brisbane, Australian rugby union hit rock bottom as a little island nation ran riot. Tonga, with more than enough aggression to make up for their international innocence, scored 4 tries to 2 in a historic victory.

Perhaps Australia should have seen it coming. They had been dubbed the 'Woeful Wallabies' after a dreadful tour of New Zealand the previous year. Tonga's free-running players soon sensed uncertainty among their hosts. Sami Latu came off his wing to score one memorable try, while the names of Mosi, Vave and Kavapalu will forever be etched into Tongan rugby history, after they too breached Australia's defences.

Following the humiliation, there was a painful inquest into how it could have happened, and much wailing about the murky depths to which Wallabies rugby had sunk. Fact-finding expeditions to Britain were organized to see what they were doing right on the other side of the world. Administrative streamlining and clearer coaching structures gave hope for a brighter future.

Sure enough, a decade later the Wallabies were back among the very best, and by 1991 Australia were official world champions. Tonga had given the Aussies a brutal wake-up call. Looking back, those four-try Pacific islanders did the Wallabies a huge favour.

Opposite: The Woeful Wallabies of 1973 went on to lose against Wales 24-0, and England 20-3. Here Australia's Mike Cocks and Rex L'Estrange tussle with England's Chris Ralston and Stack Stevens.

Bosco's Lion Beaters

Fiji 25 British Lions 21

1977 Regarded as the greatest result in Fiji rugby history, this unlikely victory against Phil Bennett's British Lions was even more deserved than the score-line suggests, since Pio Bosco Tikoisuva's rampant islanders ran in five tries to the tourists' three. They became known as 'Bosco's Lion Beaters', and the captain himself was chaired-off the field by his team-mates on the final whistle.

So how had they done it? The Lions were on their way back from a 3-1 series defeat in New Zealand, their morale dented by the narrow loss they suffered in the final test. With the likes of Bennett and Billy Beaumont in their ranks, they hardly lacked character or quality, having lost only one non-test match on tour. Therefore nothing should be taken away from the magnificent Fijians, for whom Vuate Naresia and Antonio Racika, the latter a try-scorer back in 1970 against the Barbarians, both went over twice. Joape Kuinikoro made up the list of Fiji's glory boys, with Racika converting once and Tikoisuva adding a drop goal.

Though Bennett, Beaumont and David Burcher all scored tries for the Lions, it was only the captain's three conversions and a penalty that kept the shell-shocked British in touch. Fiji have never forgotten their triumph, and rightly so.

Opposite: Phil Bennett reached new heights as a star player when he joined the British Lions on a tour of Africa, scoring a total of 103 points. Here he displays his expert skills playing for Wales in the Five Nations Championship in 1978.

Knife-Edge Victory

Graham Mourie's Grand Slam Dramatists

1978 At the sixth attempt, New Zealand finally completed a Grand Slam of victories over England, Ireland, Wales and Scotland in 1978. Graham Mourie's team deserve their place in history, though each man would readily admit that their achievement was left on a knife-edge until virtually the final whistle in Britain. Victories over England and Ireland were entertaining enough, but could not quite match the tests against Wales and Scotland for sheer drama.

In Cardiff, Wales were leading 12-10 with only sixty seconds left on the clock. The line-out that followed has been a bone of contention in both hemispheres. Andy Haden dived to the floor and the referee, Roger Quittenton, awarded the All Blacks a penalty. There were allegations of gamesmanship levelled at Haden, though Quittenton insisted later that he had blown when he saw Welshman Geoff Wheel climbing with the help of Frank Oliver's shoulder. Whatever the truth of the matter, Brian McKechnie held his nerve and kicked the vital penalty for a controversial 13-12 All Blacks victory.

Against Scotland in the last, all-important match, darkness was falling as Ian McGeechan attempted a drop goal to wipe away New Zealand's 12-9 lead. Doug Bruce charged down to save the Grand Slam, and the tourists even broke away to score at the other end so that celebrations could begin in earnest.

Opposite: England's Peter Wheeler tries to tackle New Zealand's Gary Seear, a converted lock who had a brief test career, in the game that saw them beat England 16-6 during their 1978 Grand Slam tour.

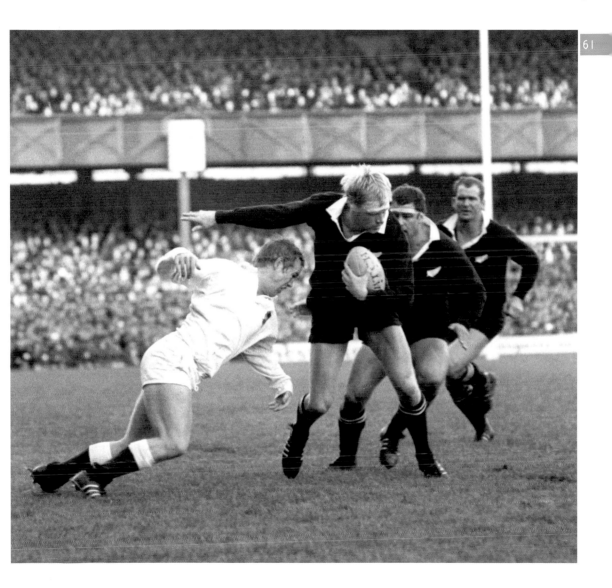

Eden Park

The Flour-Bomb Test

1981 Entire books have been written about this single match, during which a dare-devil pilot called Marx Jones and his 'bombardier in the back', Grant Cole, risked their lives to make a spectacular but dangerous protest against the evil of apartheid. Those who believed that politics should leave sport alone were incensed when a series of death-defying, low-level passes by Marx in a single-engine Cessna left Eden Park strewn with flour bombs and flares.

South Africa's tour of New Zealand had been allowed to go ahead, despite violent protests and the disruption of two earlier games. The series was in the balance at one test each when the attack came from above. 'Do you not have an air-force in this country?' demanded South Africa's captain, Wynand Klaassen, of his opponents as the bombardment intensified and the All Blacks' prop, Gary Knight, was almost knocked unconscious by one missile.

Klaassen's Springboks, who were 16-3 down at half-time, did not suffer in the onslaught, fighting their way back to 22-22. Alan Hewson landed a last-minute penalty to clinch the series for New Zealand, though the country remained divided over its conduct in having allowed South Africa to tour.

Marx Jones, the pilot whose protest went down in history, probably put it best when he said, 'There were other issues which outgrew the rugby'.

Opposite: New Zealand All Black rugby player Andy Hayden concentrates on the game as flour bombs explode on the field during the third test between New Zealand and South Africa at Eden Park, Auckland, 12 September 1981.

Max Krilich's Invincibles (LEAGUE)

Carnage Takes Game to New Level

1982 The 1982 Kangaroo tourists became the first team to win all fifteen of their fixtures in Britain, though it was the emphatic manner of victory that sent shockwaves through the north of England. The rampant Australians clocked up 423 points at an average of 28.2 per match, an incredible feat that put them a cut above all northern hemisphere pretenders.

The captain, Max Krilich, unleashed some of the most talented tourists Britain had ever seen, and hardened northern crowds were left marvelling at the skills of favoured half-backs Brett Kenny and Peter Stirling, as well as the legendary Mal Meninga and Wally Lewis.

It was during the second test at Wigan, with the Kangaroos leading 17-6 at half-time, that Lewis and Meninga combined to take the series out of reach. 'King Wally', a second-half substitute, threw a breathtaking twenty-five yard pass for Meninga to score, a piece of daring that had never been seen before in top-flight rugby league. The fact that the Australians were down to twelve men by then rubbed salt into British wounds, as did the 32-8 drubbing in the final test. There was a huge inquest in Britain after the one-sided carnage, and teams there went fully professional in an effort to catch up with the brilliant Kangaroos, who had taken the game to a new level.

'You could tell straightaway... the style of him, the way he moved.. he was just unbelievable.'
**_Tommy Bishop in reference to Steve Rogers,
Kangaroos (pictured opposite playing against
St Helens, 1982)_**

Wally Lewis (LEAGUE)

King Wally

1980s Some said he was the best rugby player they had ever seen, which explains his nickname – King Wally. A schoolboy team-mate of rugby union's awesome Ella brothers, Lewis clearly had all the talent he needed to make it big in either code. He chose League. Few could spin a pass quite as far, tackle with such brutal force or take quite such a grip of a game when he was on-song.

He played some magical cameo roles on the 1982 Kangaroos tour to Britain, but Lewis only made the fly-half spot his own the following year, for the series against New Zealand. Success in that contest led to Lewis being given the captaincy in 1984, a decision that demonstrated the selectors' new faith in him. He held on to his place in the Kangaroos side until 1991, except when injured, and played a total of thirty-three tests.

King Wally captained his country for five years, though New South Wales fans were none too thrilled to have a Queenslander running the show, particularly at the start of his reign. They even jeered Lewis when he lifted the Ashes in front of them in 1984.

However, over time, inter-State rivalry could not prevent the vast majority of Australian fans from taking Lewis to their hearts. His leadership inspired the 'Unbeatables' to another undefeated tour of Britain in 1986, and guided Australia through the three hard years it took to lift the 1988 World Cup.

Wally Lewis

Born: 1 December 1959

Place of birth: Brisbane, Australia

Caps: 34

Teams: Queensland, Wakefield Trinity, Gold Coast Seagulls, Brisbane Broncos, Australia

Mark Ella

The Wallabies' Grand Slam

1984 Some greats have to be savoured swiftly, because they retire so early that saddened fans are glad they did not blink and miss the speedy genius on show. Such a man was Mark Ella, who quit in 1984 at the age of twenty-five, having achieved all he wanted in the game he had faithfully served until that surprising moment.

His enduring achievement was to score a try against every home nation as he led Australia's Grand Slam Tour of the UK and Ireland in 1982. Ella, who often played for the Wallabies alongside his brothers, Gary and Glen, inspired three victories over the All Blacks on New Zealand soil in that same magical year. On the other side of the world, he carved through respected defences with consummate ease, helping Australia to beat England 19-3 and Ireland 16-9. The tourists then seemed to relax and move up a gear to destroy Wales 28-9 and Scotland 37-12.

Ella blended a relatively low centre of gravity with deft footwork and supreme handling skills, and at one stage he was on a par with fellow Aussie genius David Campese. As early as 1980, the gifted three-quarter had delivered a show-stopping 'around-the-body' pass that helped send Peter Grigg clear in a 26-10 win over the All Blacks in Sydney.

The party was cut short in 1984, when Ella tired of the politics that saw him replaced as Wallabies captain by Andrew Slack. The fireworks had been all too brief, but truly spectacular nonetheless.

Mark Ella

Born: 5 June 1959

Place of birth: Sydney, Australia

Caps: 25

Teams: Australia

The Battle Of Tonga

Wales On Tour

1986 On 12 June 1986, the Welsh team arrived at the Teufaiva stadium, Nuku'alofa, Tonga, thinking they were about to play in no more than a rugby match. Little did they know that the contest would more closely resemble a boxing match.

Early in the game, three Tongan forwards floored Welsh flanker Mark Brown, and suddenly the entire touring team was caught up in a mass brawl, with the notable exceptions of Malcolm Dacey and Mark Titley. Winger Adrian Hadley and number eight Phil Davies were soon laid out cold. Stuart Evans and Billy James were also down. The fight was not going well for Wales. Despite his background with South Wales Police, Bleddyn Bowen ran away from the fearsome Tongan prop, Tevita Bloomfield, and dived into the crowd. Unluckily for Bowen, the spectators threw him straight back. Though Wales cannot be said to have won the boxing match, they did somehow win what was left of the rugby, 15-7.

At the post-match dinner, Jonathan Davies was asked to treat his hosts to a quick burst of the Welsh language. As they applauded, he called them 'the dirtiest team I have ever played against'. Robert Jones later described the carnage as 'the worst brawl I have ever seen on a rugby field'.

For the record, Wales had already defeated Fiji, and beat Western Samoa on the last leg of their tour to make it a clean sweep. They were not sorry to get home.

'League is much, much more physical than Union, and that's before anyone starts breaking the rules.'

Adrian Hadley (pictured opposite)

John Kirwan (Union and League)

Dazzling Superstar

1980s John Kirwan was one of those rare, lucky players who could say that he achieved everything he wanted to, and more, in a glorious All Blacks career that saw him play sixty-three Test Matches between 1984 and 1994.

Nowhere were his graceful running skills more evident than on the greatest stage of all, at the World Cup. In 1987, the brave experiment that was known as the Inaugural World Cup needed a superstar to dazzle the crowds. In Kirwan, the tournament found its hero, and he lost no time in setting that stage alight.

In the opening match against Italy, Kirwan scored a try that is still remembered. When he caught the ball from kick-off deep in his own half, not even the brilliant three-quarter knew what would happen next. Later he explained, 'A gap opened up and I managed to beat three or four players and end up eighty yards down the pitch to score.'

It was the start of a glorious World Cup journey that saw him finish as the competition's top try-scorer with 6. He was the most exciting player on show in the team that took the trophy. Even with a hamstring injury in the final, Kirwan still managed to shut out pain and score in the victory over France.

Kirwan played a major part in a glorious unbeaten run of twenty-three matches from 1987–90, diving over for 10 tries in five tests alone against Wales and Australia in 1988. In all, he scored thirty-five times for the All Blacks before turning to rugby league for two seasons with the Auckland Warriors.

John Kirwan

Born: 16 December 1964

Place of birth: Auckland, New Zealand

Caps: 63

Teams: Auckland Warriors, New Zealand

Grant Fox

The Kicking Machine

1980s Grant Fox was the forerunner of the modern-day kicking automaton. He was so fearsome with the boot, either from a penalty or in running play, that not even the All Blacks had seen quite such a level of dependability before. Teams struggling against the New Zealanders also realized they would be punished if they tried to stifle their play illegally. In short, there was no way out. Fox seized upon such desperation to rattle up the All Blacks' points tally with unerring accuracy.

He scored an extraordinary 645 points in forty-six tests and was never more prolific than when he found himself under the spotlight on the biggest stages. At the 1987 World Cup, for example, he scored no fewer than 126 points in six matches, notching up 26 against Fiji alone, and 17 in the final against France. Not surprisingly, he finished as leading points scorer in the tournament, his kicking skills unmatched at the time in world rugby.

His master-class continued until 1993, when he scored half of New Zealand's 64 points in the series triumph over the British Lions. His last-minute kick in the first test clinched a 20-18 victory, and set the standard for his work in all three contests, the All Blacks emerging 2-1 winners.

No one anticipated that Fox's kicking record would ever be broken; however, his achievements were the inspiration a successor needed to reach even dizzier heights.

Grant Fox

Born: 6 June 1962

Place of birth: New Plymouth, New Zealand

Caps: 49

Teams: Auckland, Auckland Blues, New Zealand, New Zealand Cavaliers

All Black Magic

New Zealand Win the First World Cup

1987 No twentieth-century team won the World Cup in quite such emphatic style as New Zealand who took the inaugural tournament in 1987. Later finals sometimes turned into tense shoot-outs between nerveless goal-kickers, and the most entertaining sides did not always come out on top, but the first competition, played in Australia and New Zealand, saw one team turn on the style from start to finish. The fact that the magic was from a host country in familiar surroundings did not diminish the beauty of the rugby.

The individual exploits of John Kirwan and Grant Fox are already detailed. However, unusually, the bigger picture (of which they were just a part) was even more stunning than the individual stars.

The All Blacks ran in no fewer than 43 tries in the 1987 tournament. They clocked up 298 points in just six matches, averaging almost 50 points per match. A stunning 70-point start against Italy was bettered with a 74-point haul in another Pool B game against Fiji. Argentina conceded 46 in the last group game, Scotland 30 in the quarter-final, and Wales 49 in a one-sided semi-final. Only France kept New Zealand below 30 points, though even the score-line of 29-9 in the final was emphatic enough. By the time the All Blacks' captain, David Kirk, lifted the trophy at Eden Park, even rival fans knew his amazing team were worthy winners.

Opposite: David Kirk, pictured here holding the William Webb Ellis trophy after New Zealand's triumph, abruptly retired from competitive rugby immediately after the World Cup win to take up a Rhodes Scholarship at Worcester College, Oxford with a degree in PPE. He was awarded the MBE in 1987 for services to Rugby.

David Campese

Campo

1980s–90s David Campese is regarded as one of the greatest flare players of all time. He played a major part in his country's Rugby World Cup triumph of 1991. Not only did his famous 'goose step' often wrong-foot mesmerized opponents, but also, his taste for psychological warfare meant that rival teams were sometimes half-beaten before a match had even begun.

A maverick, Campese was also prone to the occasional catastrophic error, such as the one that cost Australia the 1989 Test Series against the British Lions. He lived on the edge and had his attempted interception in the dying minutes of the 1991 World Cup final against England been ruled a deliberate knock-on, Australia might not have gone home with the William Webb Ellis trophy.

Campese's place in history was always assured, whatever the achievements of the teams he played for. His final total of 46 international tries was a world record, beaten in only 2006. He is best remembered for the outrageous talent he oozed from every pore, his power and blistering pace and, above all, the wonderful unpredictability that helped him to become one of the greatest entertainers the rugby world has ever seen. Campese in full flight, leaving opponents for dead as he roared towards the try-line, remains one of the sport's most enduring and beautiful sights.

David Campese

Born: 21 October 1962
Place of birth: Queanbeyan, Australia
Caps: 101
Teams: Australia

Michael Jones

The Iceman

1980s–90s John Hart, New Zealand's coach when Jones was in his pomp, remembers the flanker as 'the greatest rugby player I've ever seen'. Yet the deeply religious Jones will also be remembered for his refusal to play on a Sunday.

When he did play, Jones was not slow to carve his name in history. He was the first man to score a World Cup try, against Italy in 1987, when he was crowned champion along with his team-mates. The Iceman was also the first player to score tries in two World Cups as New Zealand charged towards the 1991 semi-finals; however, the crucial match against Australia fell on a Sunday, just like two others Jones had already missed. He followed in the steps of 'Chariots of Fire' hero, Eric Liddle, and resisted any attempt to persuade him to play, insisting God had set aside Sunday as a day of rest. The All Blacks were beaten, and Jones was not selected for the 1995 World Cup in case the same thing happened again.

By then, Jones was already injury-prone, having damaged a knee in 1989 against Argentina's Pumas. Neither his spiritual beliefs nor the physical limitations of his body prevented Jones from playing fifty-five times for his country, providing the perfect link between forwards and three-quarters, and some devastating cover tackles on the opposition.

Jones was once asked how he could tackle so ruthlessly given his religious convictions. 'It is better to give than to receive', he said with a smile.

Michael Jones

Born: 8 April 1965

Place of birth: Auckland, New Zealand

Caps: 56

Teams: New Zealand, Samoa

Michael Lynagh

Prolific, Consistent and Unflappable Kicker

1980s–90s One of the greatest goal-kickers of all time, in a test career from 1984 to 1995, Michael Lynagh scored a mind-boggling 911 points for his country in seventy-two matches. He seemed unflappable, with an almost superhuman consistency in front of goal, sending out the sort of punishing message, with his pin-point strikes, that slowly sapped the spirit of the opposition.

Perhaps because he was so very dependable with the boot, it was easy to forget what a powerful and elegant fly-half he could be. He used his trademark composure to turn the course of Australia's 1991 Rugby World Cup campaign. With Nick Farr-Jones injured in the quarter-final against Ireland, Lynagh took the captain's arm-band and led his country to a seemingly impossible comeback. Only seconds of stoppage time were remaining when Lynagh hit back against what looked like Ireland's winning score and went over for his own last-gasp try to send Australia through.

Before the final against England, Lynagh had an uncharacteristic crisis of confidence in front of the posts. It said everything about his search for perfection that he managed to correct the problem in time to kick 7 vital points in a low-scoring showpiece, helping the Aussies to their first world crown.

The following year he notched a decisive 28 points against New Zealand to secure the series triumph. Feared and respected in equal measure, Lynagh was one of the most prolific goal-kickers of his generation.

Michael Lynagh

Born: 25 October 1963
Place of birth: Brisbane, Australia
Caps: 73
Teams: Queensland, Saracens, Australia

Tim Horan

Most-Capped Australian Centre

1980s–90s For a man who started out in rugby league, Tim Horan certainly left an indelible mark on the history of rugby union. Arguably the greatest centre of all time, his cutting surges through opposing defences inspired Australia to World Cup glory in 1991 and 1999. His formidable strength and deceptive pace earned him Player of the Tournament in 1999, perhaps the ultimate individual accolade in rugby. Horan's eighty test appearances for the Wallabies made him the most-capped Australian centre in their proud history.

It was the searing quality of his performances in the 1991 World Cup that sent a frightening message to rivals. In Horan, it emerged, the Aussies had a force every bit as potent as his celebrated fellow three-quarter, David Campese. Horan was perhaps a little less showy, but when the pair combined in full flight it was poetry in motion and no defensive line was immune. Their understanding seemed to reach telepathic levels at times and one of the enduring memories from Rugby World Cup 1991 was the try that virtually put paid to New Zealand's reign as the best on the planet. About to be closed down, Campese threw the ball over his shoulder without even looking to see where it was going. Horan knew, and duly collected to puncture a hole in the All Blacks' defence for a dream try. The man was a winner from head to toe.

Tim Horan

Born: 18 May 1970
Place of birth: Darlinghurst, Australia
Caps: 80
Teams: Quelomuensland Reds, Saracens, Australia

Viliami Ofahengaue

Willy

1990s Willy Ofahengaue was the raging bull who gained the hard yards and pierced armour-plated defences in a style that assured his team-mates that victory was not only possible but there for the taking.

As a youngster he could not get past one barrier, and rugby-loving Kiwis must have regretted the actions of one of their passport control officers ever since. The big flanker had been representing New Zealand schoolboys on tour to Australia in 1988 when he was refused re-entry on his Tongan passport. An outraged Ofahengaue decided that if New Zealand did not want him, he would make them pay by playing for deadly rivals Australia instead.

Big Willy did just that, and won forty-one caps for Australia between 1990 and 1998, scoring 11 tries. His wild streak made him loved and feared in equal measure, and his confidence stunned England in the 1991 World Cup final.

Much vaunted for their forward power, England's pack that year was probably the best in the world, yet it was Ofahengaue who emerged from that final head and shoulders above any other forward on the pitch. It was not the last time in a bruising and distinguished career.

'Willy' Ofahengaue

Born: 3 May 1968
Place of birth: Kolofoou, Tonga
Caps: 41
Teams: Australia

Psyched Out

Wallabies Beat England to Win World Cup

1991 Some put Australia's triumph down to the running power of rugby adventurers David Campese, Tim Horan and even Willy Ofahengaue; others credit the tactical acumen of half-back partnership Nick Farr-Jones and Michael Lynagh; but those who worked closely with England and Australia in the build-up to that final will always be convinced that the single biggest factor behind the Wallabies' defiant victory was David Campese's mouth.

Provocatively, the controversial star asked England why they continued to bore the world rigid with a forward-led game, when they had the likes of Jeremy Guscott and Rory Underwood waiting to set that same world alight outside. Love them or hate them, England's low-risk tactics had taken them all the way to the final. More of the same, the experts predicted, would see off Australia too, for all their flare. Who cared what 'Campo' said?

The answer was Will Carling. England's captain fell for Campese's psychological ploy, abandoned the tight tactics that had brushed aside all challengers, and tried to play expansive rugby in the final. It looked good but it did not quite work, partly because the English were out of practice when it came to passing out wide. Campese's taunts had hit the bullseye: instead of playing to their strengths, the English were psyched out of their moment of glory, and Australia scavenged enough ball to emerge triumphant.

'I knew that '91 was the final throw of the dice for me, which meant a lot of pressure and a lot of build-up and speculation.'

Nick Farr-Jones (pictured opposite, raising the trophy)

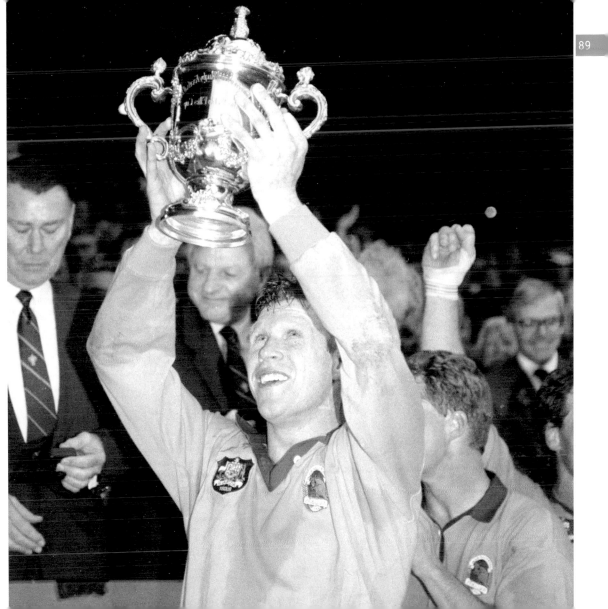

Meninga's Awesome Kangaroos

Australia Win Rugby League World Cup

1992 The tenth rugby league World Cup produced a final far more dramatic than many of the anti-climactic conclusions to previous tournaments.

The showdown between Mal Meninga's awesome Kangaroos and battling Great Britain had been four years in the making, since the competition had begun back in 1989. Australia had reached the final long before the British, who had to overcome New Zealand to earn their place. When the time came for the long-awaited showpiece, some 73,631 faces watched at Wembley Stadium (still an all-time record).

The Kangaroos had won the Ashes 2-1 earlier that year, and for a long time revenge hung in the London air. The predominantly British crowd must have thought they were about to be rewarded for turning up in such huge numbers. With twelve minutes left, their side still led 6-4 and seemed to have won the absorbing war of attrition, but they did not grasp the cool determination behind Meninga's winning habit, or how quickly a player nicknamed The Pearl would slip through their fingers. Steve Renouf, a diabetic of Aboriginal heritage, collected a timely pass from Kevin Walters and suddenly left his opponent, John Devereux, for dead. Meninga personally converted Renouf's all-important try and, despite brave British efforts to hit back, lifted the cup for his country.

'Getting him to training was a defining moment, then getting him to finish was another. We named the hill after him because he spent so much time sitting on it.'

Wayne Bennett, Steve Renouf's coach

Rugby Arrival in Emphatic Style

Western Samoa Reach World Cup Quarter-Finals

1991 '95 To understand how quickly Western Samoa (also known as Manu Samoa after a legendary tribal chief) exploded on to the international scene, it is worth remembering that they were not even invited to the inaugural Rugby World Cup in 1987.

The Samoans certainly announced their arrival in emphatic style when their turn came, because they reached the quarter-finals of the next two World Cups under the gritty guidance of their coach Bryan Williams, a former All Black.

At Cardiff Arms Park in 1991, the Welsh somehow underestimated a Western Samoa side that included Pat Lam, Frank Bunce and Stephen Bachop. Ferocious tackling and an adventurous running game gave the Samoans a platform to edge the match 16-13, one of the shocks of the tournament. Perhaps the win over Wales and a bruising, though highly respectable, 3-9 defeat to eventual winners Australia left the Samoans hung over for Scotland, who won their quarter-final 28-6.

By the next World Cup in 1995, the Samoans had become feared opponents, and England were left nursing several injuries after a bone-crunching group match in Durban. Both teams beat Italy and Argentina, but Manu Samoa then came up against South Africa in the quarter-final, and Chester Williams put away 4 tries for the eventual champions, so ending the islanders' resistance. Even so, the Samoans had been well and truly accepted among rugby's big boys.

'I have enormous love for Wales and the Welsh people. They were among the first top-tier nations to recognize the rise of Pacific Islander rugby and we share a common passion for the game.'

Pat Lam (pictured opposite, centre, tackling Scotland in the 1991 World Cup)

Man-Mountain Causes Chaos

Jonah Lomu Destroys England at World Cup

1995 Before their Cape Town semi-final with New Zealand, England manager Jack Rowell was adamant that either of the Underwood brothers, Tony or Rory, would be able to handle a man-mountain called Jonah Lomu, who was already taking the World Cup by storm. Though the Underwoods were nippy wingers, neither was famous for solid tackling. Rowell remained unconcerned, claiming there would be plenty of support from the rest of the England team when it came to bringing the giant down. All Blacks captain Sean Fitzpatrick smiled when he heard about England's confidence and muttered, 'I wouldn't like to be in the Underwood brothers' shoes'.

As it turned out, Fitzpatrick had foreseen the chaos that would follow, and Rowell had been living in fantasy land. Lomu swatted Tony Underwood aside, ran over Mike Catt at full-back, and made a mockery of anyone else who tried to prevent his opening score. Even then England did not seem to learn their lesson as Lomu ran riot and powerful forwards bounced off him like rain drops. The first half was a one-sided embarrassment. By the final whistle Lomu had pocketed 4 tries and the All Blacks had won 45-29. Will Carling, who had scored a couple in a token English comeback, declared afterwards, 'Lomu is a freak'. No one has ever destroyed a top team single-handedly like that before or since.

Jonah Lomu

Born: 12 May 1975

Place of birth: Auckland, New Zealand

Caps: 63

Teams: Counties Manukau, Wellington, Cardiff Blues, North Harbour, Hurricanes, Chiefs, Blues, New Zealand

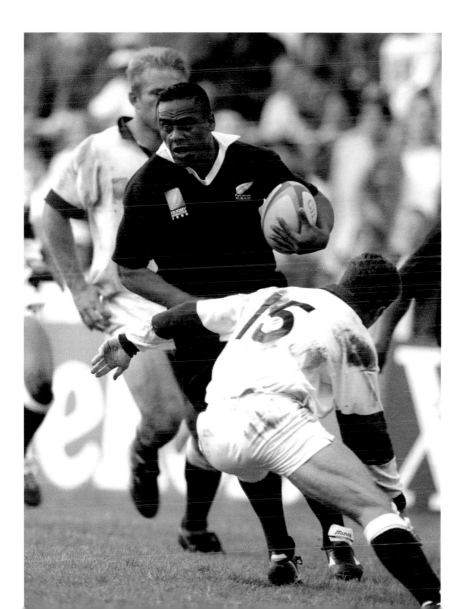

Rugby Immortality

Sean Fitzpatrick's Triumphant All Blacks

1996 The key to Sean Fitzpatrick's stunning success in 1996 almost certainly lay in what he had been forced to endure the previous year. His team were struck down by suspicious food poisoning hours before facing hosts South Africa in the World Cup final. Many thought it was the difference between victory and the narrow defeat they suffered. Then South African Rugby Football Union (SARFU) President, Louis Luyt, boasted at the post-match dinner that the Springboks would have won the first two World Cups as well, had they been allowed to play in them.

Fitzpatrick was easily motivated the next time the countries met. Having scored 6 stunning tries in a Tri-Nations rout of Australia, the All Blacks beat the Springboks 15-11 in Christchurch, but it was when Fitzpatrick returned to South Africa that the anger really started to kick in. Down 18-6 to the Springboks in Cape Town, he inspired his troops to fight back for an extraordinary 29-18 victory.

What turned out to be the 1996 series clincher in South Africa, the first in New Zealand's history, was a 33-26 second-test victory at altitude in the Loftus Versfeld stadium. When the final whistle blew, exhausted All Blacks collapsed all over the field, but they knew they had achieved rugby immortality. Fitzpatrick had secured his revenge and reward for his superb leadership.

Opposite: Sean Fitzpatrick runs at Scotland's Doddie Weir and Barry Stewart in a match the All Blacks won 36-12, laying the ground for their upcoming success in August against the Springboks.

Tonga's Greatest Home Result

Tonga 20 France 16

1999 Less than five months after this 16 June date with Tonga, France produced one of the most dazzling performances of all time in order to reach the 1999 World Cup final.

Daunting as they were, France's semi-final opponents at Twickenham, New Zealand, did not have anyone quite as youthfully ferocious as Tonga's Siua 'Josh' Taumalolo. The versatile three-quarter, comfortable at full-back or centre, was already building himself a reputation as an explosive try-scorer before the fancied French arrived on Tonga. He had ripped Leicester apart the previous year with a hat-trick and nine conversions as the Barbarians handed the Midlanders their record defeat, 73-19. Taumalolo set about the French as though they too had no reputation worth respecting, which, of course, could not have been further from the truth.

Only one team turned on the style in Nuku'alofa though, and it was not the more-celebrated three-quarter line orchestrated by the famous Christophe 'Titou' Lamaison. Taumalolo cut through for two tries, Taunaholo Taufahana added another and, despite Olivier Sarramoa's reply, Tonga had registered their greatest result at home.

The fearsome Taumalolo was sent off in the World Cup later that year for a high tackle on Jonah Lomu; but when Tonga's wild man got it right, as he did against France, he was simply too hot to handle.

Siua Taumalolo

Born: 8 July 1976
Place of birth: Tonga
Caps: 15
Teams: Ebbw Vale, Pacific Islanders, Tonga

Andrew Mehrtens

Tri-Nations' Highest Scorer

1990s Goal-kickers do not come more prolific than Andrew Mehrtens, who achieved what many had thought impossible when he passed Grant Fox's all-time points record for the All Blacks. He is also the highest scorer in Tri-Nations history, a further testament to his nerve under pressure.

By the time the unflappable Mehrtens finished at test level, he had clocked up 967 points, a phenomenal tally considering his rivalry with Carlos Spencer for New Zealand's fly-half spot.

For Canterbury, Mehrtens even reached four figures, ending on 1056 points to underline his immaculate accuracy. He tasted World Cup disappointment in South Africa during his first year at international level, but had his revenge in 1996 when he played a major role in the All Blacks' first ever series win there.

By the time World Cup 1999 came around, he was so confident that he encouraged the Twickenham crowd to jeer him while he was preparing for goal-kicks, because he claimed the hostility would make him perform even better.

Never the most flamboyant of runners by All Blacks standards, he will be remembered above all for his mastery when the posts were in his sights and the records he sent tumbling.

Andrew Mehrtens

Born: 28 April 1973

Place of birth: Durban, South Africa

Caps: 70

Teams: Canterbury, Crusaders, Harlequins, New Zealand

LEGEND

Nobody's Perfect

John Eales Leads Australia to World Cup Glory

1999 The nickname his team-mates gave John Eales said everything about his international record. They called him 'Nobody', a witty reference to the phrase 'nobody's perfect'. When a giant second row, some two metres tall, turns out to be a superb goal-kicker as well as an inspirational leader, this is as close to sporting perfection as possible. Eales was the biggest single reason why Australia won two World Cups in the 1990s and he personally lifted the second of those Webb Ellis trophies in 1999.

Dan Crowley, Phil Kearns, Jason Little and Tim Horan also enjoyed return journeys to glory in Britain. However it was the towering presence of Eales that made the 1999 success look so straightforward.

Australia won all their Pool E matches, beating Romania, Ireland and the USA. They coasted past Wales in the quarter-final and overcame their biggest challenge against South Africa. The comparative comfort of their 35-12 win over France in the final was further testament to Eales' impeccable leadership. When 'Nobody' raised the cup above his head, it was his finest hour in a ten-year, eighty-six-test career that saw him score 189 points. Just perfect, you might say.

John Eales

Born: 27 June 1970
Place of birth: Brisbane, Australia
Caps: 86
Teams: Queensland Reds, Australia

Matt Burke

Worth His Weight in Gold

1990s–2000s Matt Burke has secured his place in history as one of the finest full-backs the game has seen. A powerful runner, he has made a significant contribution to the adventurous rugby that has brought Australia so many rewards. In 1996, for example, Burke scored one of the most memorable tries of the professional era when he used an outrageous dummy to burst past half the New Zealand team on a seventy-metre dash to the Brisbane line.

However, it is his goal-kicking that has helped Burke to make his mark in the record books. If John Eales provided the leadership during the Wallabies' 1999 World Cup triumph, it was Burke who supplied the points. He scored 24 against South Africa in the semi-final and 25 against France in the final. The previous year he had scored all 24 points for Australia against New Zealand at the MCG (Melbourne Cricket Ground), setting a world record against the All Blacks in the process.

Burke is the fifth-highest international points scorer of all time, second only behind Andrew Mehrtens in the Tri-Nations tournament. For the most points scored in tests on a single tour, Burke set a new record in 1996, when he scored 74 on the Wallabies' tour to Europe. No wonder people said he was worth his weight in gold.

Matt Burke

Born: 26 March 1973

Place of birth: Sydney, Australia

Caps: 82

Teams: Newcastle Falcons, Waratahs, Australia

George Gregan

Appointed to the Order of Australia

1990s–2000s Few have given longer, or more distinguished, service in the international arena than George Gregan. This inspirational scrum-half won his first cap with the Wallabies back in 1994. By 5 November 2005, he had amassed a world-record 115 caps, passing Jason Leonard's landmark as he led Australia out to play France in Marseilles.

A World Cup winner in 1999, Gregan's busy rugby brain and darting breaks were the catalyst for some of the Wallabies' finest sweeping moves. He was a threat whenever he had so much as a sniff of the try-line, and a high-point came when he scored an important try in the 1999 quarter-final showdown with hosts Wales.

Two years later, John Eales retired from international rugby and Gregan was his natural successor as Australia captain. He led his country to the World Cup final against England in 2003, taking his team on a controversial lap of honour after Australia's superb semi-final victory over New Zealand. Some said those premature celebrations gave England the psychological advantage for the final, but it was typical of Gregan's spontaneity and love for the game.

When he captained the Wallabies for a fifty-sixth time against New Zealand in the Bledisloe Cup during 1996, he had led his country on more occasions than Eales and was appointed to the Order of Australia for his achievements in the game.

George Gregan (pictured opposite, right)

Born: 19 April 1973
Place of birth: Lusaka, Zambia
Caps: 127
Teams: Brumbies, Australia

Waisale Serevi

The Magician

1990s–2000s It is hard to imagine a more exhilarating rugby vision than Waisale Tikoisolomoni Serevi in full flight. The fifteen-a-side game was not his speciality, though he was still capped thirty-nine times by Fiji, and played for Leicester Tigers in England as a utility back under Australian coach Bob Dwyer.

It is as a Sevens player that Serevi will never be forgotten. He was already a legend long before he came out of retirement and won Fiji the 2005 Sevens World Cup at the ripe old age of thirty-seven, adding to his first Melrose Cup in 1997, and making Fiji the first nation to win it twice.

Serevi was also at the epicentre of the explosive magic that propelled Fiji to three successive undefeated years at the Hong Kong Sevens in the early 1990s. His blistering pace and mesmerizing trickery won him three 'Most Valuable Player' awards in Hong Kong, and his trophy cabinet is packed with other honours, such as a gold medal from the 2001 World Games and two silver medals from the Commonwealth Games.

Serevi's balance, unpredictability and sheer genius for blowing holes in defences made him one of the greatest rugby-sevens artists of all time. He is also probably without equal as a showman and conjurer of breathtaking tries.

Waisale Serevi

Born: 20 May 1968
Place of birth: Suva, Fiji
Caps: 40
Teams: Leicester Tigers, Stade Montois, Fiji

Christian Cullen

Immense Speed and Side-Step to Die For

1990s–2000s They say Christian Cullen, the only man to rival Serevi as the king of the Sevens circuit, did not quite fulfil his potential in the fifteen-a-side game, that he was unlucky with injuries and never starred in a World Cup. It may even be true, but one glance at the record books tells a very different story. Cullen is number-one try-scorer of all time for the All Blacks, with an awesome 46 on the records. Only three conversions supplemented a points total that stopped on 236, leaving him fifth in the scoring charts. Those above him – Andrew Mehrtens, Grant Fox, Dan Carter and Carlos Spencer – have all got there by kicking points as well as scoring tries. What the statistics tell us, therefore, is that no one in the All Blacks' history could run quite like Christian Cullen.

His record number of tries at the Hong Kong Sevens in 1996 led many to believe he would become one of the game's greatest legends. He had immense speed and a side-step to die for. Injury took away some of those gifts and, although he was built to run like the wind, he was not the toughest or most durable player the game has known. Despite that, Cullen's ruthless destruction of Tri-Nations defences left one question: since he remains New Zealand's top try-scorer, what would he have been able to achieve had he really fulfilled his potential, steered clear of injury and been able to command World Cup stages? The mind boggles.

Christian Cullen

Born: 12 February 1976
Place of birth: Paraparaumu, New Zealand
Caps: 61
Teams: Hurricanes, Munster, New Zealand,
New Zealand Maori

A Thrilling Series

Australia Beat British Lions for First Time

2001 Australia took advantage of the Lions' identity crisis to come from behind and win the series 2-1, their first ever triumph over normally formidable tourists. This was the first time the Lions had been known as 'The British and Irish Lions' and the first time their coach had not hailed from one of the four 'Home Nations'. Graham Henry was not popular among the Lions players, some of whom complained that they were overworked. Indifferent morale in the Lions' camp did not stop them drawing first blood in the series, but the Wallabies hit back with a 35-14 victory in the second test in Melbourne. Joe Roff powered in for 2 tries, and the prolific Matthew Burke scored the rest of Australia's points with a try, conversion and six penalties.

So it was all down to the deciding third test in Sydney, where Jonny Wilkinson became the British scapegoat with a very uncharacteristic three penalty misses. Daniel Herbert finished off two scintillating Australian moves, and John Eales inspired Justin Harrison to a superb test debut. Wilkinson kept the Lions in the hunt by converting his own try and, in the end, it was down to a test of nerve between the kickers. Burke came out on top with two crucial penalties in the last twelve minutes, and even Lions' skipper, Martin Johnson, said, 'We've got no excuses, it was a thrilling series and Australia deserved to win it'.

'A confident side respects the opposition. An arrogant side doesn't. I hope that remains the Wallaby motto for as long as they're around. I still say the Lions have been the best team we've played, but my greatest memories will be the composure shown by this Wallaby side under extreme conditions.'

The then Wallaby coach Rod Macqueen

Fiji's Game Gels

Fiji Become Pacific Rim Champions

2001 In July 2001, battle between Fiji and deadly rivals Western Samoa was rejoined in the final of the Pacific Rim Tournament in Tokyo. Western Samoa's World Cup adventures in the 1990s had often left Fiji in the shade, and this was a chance to redress the balance. Fiji took it, thanks to a 23-point tally from goal-kicker Nicky Little, and a try under the posts by Alfie Uluinayo. Little had turned pressure into points every time the opportunity arose and Fiji led from start to finish to emerge as winners 28-17.

Injuries to both Samoan locks had made the Samoan task harder, but their assistant coach, Michael Jones, was not making excuses. 'Fiji made things gel, and Samoa is still on a learning curve,' he claimed. 'We hope to change from a good team into a great team.'

Fiji's captain, Greg Smith, summed up his sense of triumph when he said, 'There is a perception that Fiji play in Samoa's shadow, but in this final we proved we are their equal, and this year Fiji stands alone in Pacific rugby'. It was the last Pacific Rim Tournament but by no means the end of the island rivalries. The Pacific Five Nations was born in 2006 and turned into the Pacific Nations Cup in time for 2007. Rugby, always evolving, remains fiercely healthy in the region.

Opposite: Fiji's Nicky Little in 1999, playing against Italy in the Tornei Dei Quarti. Little has gone on to become the Pacific Regions Top Point Scorer, with 60 caps and 599 points.

All Blacks Win Grand Slam

One of All Blacks' Most Successful Rugby Seasons

2005 When New Zealand beat Scotland 29-10 at Murrayfield, they completed not only their first United Kingdom Grand Slam since 1978 but also one of the most successful seasons in rugby history. The All Blacks had won the Tri-Nations, whitewashed the British Lions, demolished Wales and Ireland, seen off England at Twickenham, and romped to a suitable climax against the Scots.

Their winger, Rico Gear, was the star of the show in that final match against Scotland, scoring two of New Zealand's four tries to add to his devastating hat-trick against Wales. Under the guidance of coach Graham Henry and captain Tana Umaga, it looked as though there were any number of players who could step forward to act the hero should the need arise.

The twelve tests the All Blacks played that year, starting with a 91-0 thrashing of Fiji in Albany, resulted in just one defeat, to South Africa in Cape Town. It was only a temporary lapse, because they hit back to take the Tri-Nations before humiliating Sir Clive Woodward's British Lions 3-0.

Unlike the 2001 Lions team he had coached, this New Zealand squad realized Henry's rugby vision. The secret, Henry said, was simple, 'Play the game at a tempo and skill level that your opponents can't compete with'. More easily said than done – unless you were an All Black in 2005.

'At the moment they are undoubtedly the strongest side in the world … But it doesn't mean to say people think they're invincible and unbeatable.'

Scotland coach Frank Hadden puts things into perspective…

Andrew Johns (LEAGUE)

Joey

1990s–2000s Andrew Johns is one of those rare sportsmen who achieve legendary status long before the end of their career. The Australian half-back has two World Cup winners' medals, from 1995 and 2000. In the first of those tournaments not only was he voted Most Valuable Player, but he also won Man of the Match in the final, a 16-8 victory over England. In the second, he spearheaded a rousing finish as the Kangaroos rattled up 40 points against New Zealand, with the help of 4 late tries.

It is strange to think that Joey almost quit the game between those triumphs, travelling to the Philippines for a surfing holiday as he considered his future. Johns saw so much poverty along the way that he decided it would be wrong to squander his own good fortune and went back to ruling the world of rugby league. His newfound passion for his profession was never more evident than when his Australian team, Newcastle Knights, were due to face Manley in the 1997 Grand Final. Johns was warned he might die if he tried to play with two broken ribs and a punctured lung, sustained only a fortnight earlier. Not only did he defy the doom merchants but he also set up the winning try with seconds to spare.

He was the inspiration behind the Kangaroos' comeback against the British in 2001, when they trailed in the series before storming back to win 2-1. Johns won the second of his Golden Boots as International Rugby League Player of the Year in 2001, a feat only recently equalled by Darren Lockyer.

Andrew Johns

Born: 19 May 1974

Place of birth: Kurri Kurri, Australia

Caps: 21

Teams: Newcastle Knights, Warrington, New South Wales, Australia

Stacey Jones (LEAGUE)

The Little General

2000s Stacey Jones was not blessed with the most imposing physique but that did not stop him, known as 'The Little General', from becoming the most influential Kiwi rugby league player of his generation. He so nearly inspired his country to World Cup glory in 1995, when New Zealand forced Australia into extra time in their semi-final, before going down to the eventual tournament winners. He was more successful during series wins over Great Britain in 1996 and 1998, winning Player of Series in the north of England in 1998 after a sparkling set of displays.

Australia were again too powerful in the World Cup final of 2000 but Jones always had a knack of producing the most memorable magic, even in games where he finished on the losing side. So it was in 2002, when he led Auckland Warriors to the Grand Final and scored a dazzling try despite defeat. He was on target again that year in the final test against Great Britain, even though a 16-10 win allowed the hosts to draw the series.

Such performances earned Jones the coveted Golden Boot award for International Rugby League Player of the Year. His Australian half-back rival, Andrew Johns, admitted, 'He had a better season than me and deserved it.'

Jones was anything but a loser by nature, and he came out of retirement to inspire New Zealand to a stunning Tri-Nations triumph in 2005. 'To be there with the boys and win was amazing,' he said at the time. He finally retired again after Australia took the same title back the following year.

Stacey Jones

Born: 7 May 1976

Place of birth: Auckland, New Zealand

Caps: 35

Teams: Les Catalans Dragons, New Zealand Kiwis

Kiwis Defeat Australia for First Time in Half a Century

New Zealand Win Tri-Nations (LEAGUE)

2005 When New Zealand inflicted Australia's first defeat in a test series for twenty-seven years by winning the 2005 Tri-Nations, players at opposite ends of their careers were the architects of the success story. While winger Manu Vatuvei won his first cap only at the start of the Tri-Nations, Stacey Jones had come out of retirement. The latter was coaxed back into action by New Zealand coach Brian McLennon for the opening games to be played in Australasia, but something clicked and Jones also went to England, flying back around the world to see the birth of his son before returning to play a pivotal role in the historic final alongside the nineteen-year-old Vatuvei.

Both men knew they were on to a good thing when the Kiwis defeated Australia by 38-28 at the Telstra Stadium in Sydney for the first time in half a century. The records kept tumbling as New Zealand thrashed Great Britain 42-26 at Loftus Road, West London, their highest score against that opponent.

It was in the final against Australia where rookie Vatuvei and veteran Jones combined to inflict the Kiwis' record-equalling win over their deadliest rivals. The 24-0 triumph represented the first time the Kangaroos had not scored for twenty years, and a margin of victory to sit proudly alongside the 49-25 win in Brisbane almost fifty years earlier. Jones kicked high to drop 'bombs' on the Aussie wingers, a tactic that earned Vatuvei his first try. Within five minutes he had a second, rounding off a breakaway move in the corner. Jones kicked 4 goals and, for a year at least, the young and old men of New Zealand had reduced Australia to ruins.

'We didn't give ourselves a chance, we never put ourselves in the game and they played tremendously well ... we just didn't make it a contest, they were in control all game.'

Kangaroo coach Wayne Bennett

Darren Lockyer's Golden Winner

Tri-Nations Final, Australia V New Zealand (LEAGUE)

2006 One of the most dramatic denouements in rugby league history was played out in Sydney in November, 2006. The Tri-Nations final was to be decided by a 'Golden Point' for the first time, after old rivals Australia and New Zealand were all square at 12-12 after normal time. The next to score in any shape or form won the title for his country. A big game, a big stage and now a cliffhanger of a moment, crying out for a strong character to take a starring role.

Enter Darren Lockyer, the gravel-voiced Australian stand-off, who had, only days earlier, received the Golden Boot as rugby league's best player. Now, when it really mattered, we were about to see why.

Much of the credit for Lockyer's moment of glory must go to Jonathan Thurston, whose telling break left the Kiwis vulnerable. Up popped Lockyer to catch Thurston's well-timed pass and as soon as he dived over Australia were champions. 'You couldn't have written a better script,' said Lockyer afterwards, delighted but typically self-contained. He was right. The Golden Point system allowed New Zealand no comeback, but the tension it had created proved a winner – as had Lockyer's killer score.

'That's one of the toughest games I've played in my whole career. To come away with a win like that is why I play football, I love it.'

Forward Willie Mason

Private Dancers

Haka War in The Land of My Fathers

2006 A few hours after the drama in Sydney, there was a confrontation of a sadder kind on the other side of the world at the Millennium Stadium, Cardiff. The 72,500 fans present for Wales v New Zealand were denied the chance to see and hear the emotionally charged Haka, the All Blacks' famous war dance. Instead, the tourists performed their traditional pre-match ritual in the bowels of the stadium, where only a few cameramen could witness the event.

What on earth had happened? The Welsh Rugby Union claimed to have consulted Maori chiefs (Kaumatua) before deciding to answer the Haka with their own anthem, Hen Wlad Fy Nhadau (Land of My Fathers). They claimed the Haka was designed to invite just such a response from the opposition. When the All Blacks got wind of the plan they were having none of it. Both sides refused to back down, so the New Zealanders came up with a solution that seemed mean-spirited to their hosts – they became 'private dancers'.

Many outside New Zealand believe the All Blacks are excessively precious about protecting the psychological advantage the Haka offers. Conversely, the All Blacks argue that the Haka is a wonderful gift to the world game and it should not be undermined. The row rumbles on.

'The haka is about where we come from as New Zealanders and it's about what feels right for us.'

All Blacks captain Richie McCaw

Dan Carter

If Anyone Can, Dan Can

2000s Already, going into 2007, Dan Carter had run and kicked his way to third in the all-time New Zealand scoring charts behind Andrew Mehrtens and Grant Fox. Could he eventually be the man to beat Mehrtens' amazing tally? If anyone can, Dan can.

He was voted Player of the Year at the International Rugby Board awards in 2005 and was widely recognized as the world's best fly-half again in 2006. 'It is pretty humbling when you receive an award like that,' he said that year. Such modesty does not stop him from dreaming about rugby immortality and, with his outrageous skills, it is only right that he does so.

'The truth is, I'm not satisfied with just being an All Black,' he was quoted as saying in late 2006. 'I'd like to be remembered as an All Black great, and you can't achieve that in a couple of seasons.'

Maybe not, but Carter has done enough already to convince people that, barring injury, he will achieve his ambition and then some. In some people's eyes, he is already there. In many ways he represents the future of Oceania rugby – the best there is. As Dan Carter continues to write his own story, he provides a fitting entry to end the section.

Dan Carter

Born: 5 March 1982
Place of birth: Leeston, New Zealand
Caps: 35
Teams: New Zealand

EUROPE

Europe remains something of a rugby enigma. For all the glories of French flare, the ability of European teams to hit their very best form when it really matters remains a rare treat in the modern-day game.

England, founders of rugby, managed to achieve consistent power all over the field in order to win the union game's Rugby World Cup in 2003. It was Europe's only triumph so far. Historically, the British Lions have sometimes hit sublime, uninhibited heights away from the confines of their own shores. Meanwhile, the Welsh had no need for travel to play with adventure in the days of Barry John and Gareth Edwards. In recent years, the marauding passions of the Irish and Scots have been challenged by the arrival of free-flowing Italy in the new Six Nations, a tournament still loved worldwide for its dramatic twists and turns.

Despite their sparkling history, Europe's finest in both codes are in danger of falling behind the giants of Oceania in the twenty-first century.

Rugby's Inventor

William Webb Ellis Runs with the Ball

1823 It is not known exactly why a boy called William Webb Ellis picked up the ball during a match at Rugby School in 1823, but his friends may not have been impressed. Football meant just that – using your feet to kick the ball.

In the mayhem that followed, the boys of Rugby School realized how much fun they could have with the game that Webb Ellis had unexpectedly created. It was a thrill to run with the ball, to test one's strength against others' and to meet a more physical challenge.

The Webb Ellis Stone at Rugby School describes the boy's sudden rush of blood to the head rather appropriately. Part of the inscription reads '... who with a fine disregard for the rules of football as played in his time first took the ball in his arms and ran with it, thus originating the distinctive feature of the rugby game...'.

Nearly two hundred years later, the game of rugby is loved the world over and big tournaments attract millions of viewers. Webb Ellis could not have imagined what he had started on that defining day, or indeed that rugby union's most prized trophy would be named after him. The rule-breaking schoolboy would probably break into a mischievous grin if he could see how the story has developed.

William Webb Ellis

Born: 24 November 1806   **Died**: 24 January 1872
Place of birth: Lancashire, England

LEGEND

First International

Scotland v England

1871 Being thoroughly tired of losing to England at Association Football, a group of Scottish players saw their country's 1-0 defeat to the 'auld' enemy in 1870 as the last straw. In a challenge to England, published in *The Scotsman* and *Bell's Life* journals, the Scots explained how unfair they felt it was to play the English under rules that were not popular north of the border.

'...With a view of really testing what Scotland can do against an England team we, as representatives of the football interests of Scotland, hereby challenge any team selected from the whole of England to play us a match, twenty-a-side, Rugby rules ... If it be entered into we can promise England a hearty welcome and a first-rate match...'

They could not promise to decide on a scoring system in time for the game. In that first ever international rugby match, played on the cricket field of the Edinburgh Academy on 27 March 1871, Scotland won by a try and a goal to a solitary try. The English can gain some comfort from the fact that their team won a return at the Kennington Oval, London, in the following year.

Opposite: The Scotland line-up for the first international match, including the two scorers Angus Buchanan (far left) and William Cross (middle row, fourth from right).

LANDMARK

Beginnings of Rugby League

Northern Union Founded

1895 A meeting at the George Hotel, Huddersfield, in late August 1895, irreversibly changed the face of rugby. Delegates from over twenty clubs in the north of England came together because they felt they had to take drastic action. Three years earlier, the southern-based Rugby Football Union (RFU) had charged several northern clubs with 'professionalism' following persistent rumours that players were paid for playing amateur matches. The accused clubs tried to explain that there was a need to make 'broken time' compensation payments to players who lost wages, either while playing or recovering from injuries sustained on the field of play. The RFU refused to accept this, so the George Hotel gave birth to the Northern Rugby Football Union. The delegates worked quickly, already knowing what had to be done before they arrived, and the first 'rugby league' matches were played on 7 September 1895. The Pall Mall Gazette announced coldly: 'Professional Rugby League set in on Saturday – no deaths reported.'

In fact, rugby union rules were still very much in evidence and line-outs were not dropped until two years later. The term Rugby League was not officially adopted by the Northern Union until 1922.

Opposite: Oldham, winners of the 1904–05 Rugby League Championship.

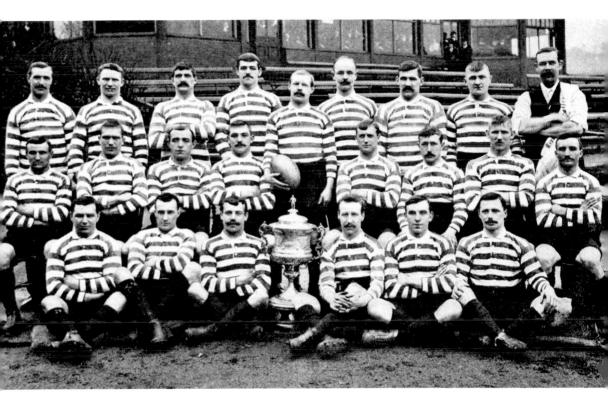

Secured with Style

England's First Back-to-Back Grand Slams

1913–14 It would be unfair to consider England's pre-war achievement without first paying tribute to the Welsh, who won the first back-to-back Grand Slams in European rugby history, in 1908 and 1909. Even though it was, at the time, officially a Home Nations tournament, the Welsh also played and beat France in those years, and Grand Slam status was duly granted. The English must also acknowledge the Welsh origins of their star half-back, Dave Davies, born in Pembroke in 1890, who provided the inspiration for England's back-to-back Grand Slams in 1913 and 1914 (by which time the tournament was called the Five Nations).

In 1913 it was England's winger, Vincent Coates, with 6 tries including a hat-trick against France, who ran riot. Their flanker, 'Cherry' Pillman, blasted holes in opposing packs with 4 tries of his own on the way to that first Grand Slam. Ultimately, it was an Australian-born prop called 'Bruno' Brown who scored the only try, and Grand Slam clincher, in the final 1913 match, a 3-0 win over Scotland at Twickenham.

In 1914, tries by Brown and Pillman edged out Wales 10-9, before a winger called Cyril Lowe burst on to the scene. He scored a double against Ireland, and hat-tricks against Scotland and France. He was bettered in that final, historic 39-13 rout of France in Paris, by a centre named Ronald Poulton-Palmer who dived over for 4 tries. Back-to-back Grand Slams could not have been secured with more style. England's extraordinary winning run might well have continued had it not been for the outbreak of World War I, after which only four of the 1914 team played again for their country. Some of England's finest players lost their lives in the trenches.

Opposite: England's 1914 team, with Cyril Lowe (back row, fourth from left), Cherry Pillman (front row, second from left), Ronald Poulton-Palmer (front row, fourth from left) and Dave Davies (front row, far right).

LANDMARK

Wavell Wakefield

Baron Wakefield of Kendal or 'Wakers'

1920s William Wavell Wakefield shaped forward play as we know it today. Baron Wakefield of Kendal, as he later became known ('Wakers' to his team-mates), saw the weakness of the haphazard way scrums were formed by throwing groups of forwards together in whatever order they arrived on the scene. Wakefield decided that specialist positions for the forwards would improve the game, with each member of the pack given a specific position and function, as we know today.

Possibly because he was a flanker, Wakers did not limit his one-man rugby revolution to specifying positions and functions for the forwards. He was dissatisfied with the pack's static approach, and increased forward mobility to develop the art of loose play. Fly-halves have Wakefield to thank for the painful tradition of being flattened by a speedy open-side flanker if they take too long over a decision.

He was very much a man ahead of his time and his innovations helped to bring England great success. He played in the Grand-Slam-winning sides of 1921, 1923 and 1924. His thirty-one caps between 1920 and 1927 (thirteen as captain) remained a record until another powerful forward, Billy Beaumont, improved on them more than half a century later.

Wavell Wakefield (pictured being tackled)

Born: 10 March 1898   **Died**: 12 August 1983
Place of birth: Beckenham, England
Caps: 31
Teams: Harlequins, England

LEGEND

Jean Galia

Founding Father of French Rugby League

1930s Jean Galia, an ex-rugby union international and champion boxer, provided the energy and leadership when rugby league gained its first foothold in France in 1934. The split was precipitated (as in England) when some of the top rugby union players were accused of accepting money to play. The game's guardians across the channel made allegations of professionalism against the French national team and they were suspended from the Five Nations Championship.

Galia and several other outraged French internationals had either heard about, or witnessed, Australia's 63-13 thrashing of England in Paris the year before – the first time rugby league had been seen in France. Defection to rugby league seemed like a natural step, especially when the northern clubs of England were only too happy to host a tour. So Galia led France on a six-match trip to England, where they even managed to win at Hull. The result helped to convince the English to go to Paris in April of the same year, where twenty thousand curious spectators watched the international game, with England edging it 32-21. Following this, the French Rugby League took off and before World War II, the French had formed 225 clubs and beaten England and Wales to win the European Championship.

Jean Galia

Born: 20 March 1905   **Died**: 17 January 1949
Place of birth: Ille-sur-Tet
Caps: 20
Teams: France

Opposite: The French team lined up to play more rugby league in England, at Leeds in 1947.

LEGEND

Prince Obolensky

Russian Aristocrat in England Shirt

1930s Resourceful rugby administrators often find a way to bend the nationality rules when a player is good enough is not a modern phenomenon. In the first week of January 1936, Prince Alexander Obolensky was selected to play for England against the All Blacks. His parents had fled to England after the Russian Revolution in 1917 but Obolensky was not even a British citizen at the turn of the year in question. No matter; 'Obo' had played for Oxford University and shown himself to be an elegant winger with speed. He was going to be a British citizen and whether it happened before or after the match against New Zealand was of little concern to the 70,000 spectators who packed Twickenham along with the Prince of Wales.

Far from being overawed by the occasion, the Russian aristocrat in the England shirt showed blistering pace down the right wing to round the All Blacks' defence and ground the ball with just a hint of a triumphant hand raised in the air. A second beauty of a try followed, and newsreel pictures captured the key moments as the home side won 13-0.

While making history, the prince on the pitch also delighted his counterpart in the stands as well as the other cheering England fans. This was England's first victory over New Zealand – and there was only one hero. He added three more caps later that year, but scored no more tries. Tragically, Obolensky was killed during Royal Air Force flight training in 1940.

Prince Obolensky

Born: 17 February 1916 **Died**: 29 March 1940

Place of birth: St Petersburg, Russia

Caps: 4

Teams: Leicester Tigers, Rosslyn Park, England

LEGEND

Gus Risman (LEAGUE)

Indomitable Career Spanning Four Decades

1930–50s Many players become legends if they score more than a thousand first-class points and stick around for more than a decade. Augustus John Risman scored 4,052 points, a total he would have happily increased had World War II not interrupted his scoring, and he remained at the top of his game for more than a quarter of a century.

He was 41 when he captained Workington Town to their 1952 Challenge Cup triumph over Featherstone Rovers at Wembley, and notched up the first of three crucial kicks in the first minute. At the time, Risman must have experienced a sense of déjà vu, because back in 1938 he had been carried aloft by his team-mates as he paraded the same trophy for the fans. The rest of the team were pictured smoking celebratory cigarettes but Risman was the exception and his dedication to fitness helped him to go on so long.

Cardiff-born of Latvian parents, Risman won eighteen caps for Wales and even played for England in the first international against France in Paris, in 1934. He also played seventeen times for Great Britain, and his proudest moment came in 1946 when he captained the 'Indomitables' Down Under. The tour was the first in any major sport after World War II, and the team earned its name not by its highly effective performances against Australia and the rest, but due to their transport for the long voyage – the aircraft carrier, HMS Indomitable. The apt title suits Risman's career, which spanned four decades, from 1929 to 1954.

Gus Risman

Born: 1911   **Died**: 17 October 1994

Place of birth: Cardiff

Caps: 36

Teams: Salford, Workington, Wales, Great Britain

LEGEND

Jackie Kyle

Ireland's First Grand Slam

1948 Long before the sports-loving people of Northern Ireland learned to adore the football legend, George Best, another Belfast Boy sparked similar hero worship. Jackie Kyle was only twenty-two when he became the architect of Ireland's finest moment in its long rugby history.

In 1948, Ireland embarked on their Five Nations campaign with a trip to Paris, where few, if any, of their players had been before. 'There was great excitement in the Stade Colombes, and we did really well winning 13-6 against a big French team.'

Six long weeks later there was a nail-biter at Twickenham, after the Irish had started in rampant mood to eleven points ahead. Kyle later recalled: 'I went over for a try in the right-hand corner but then I gave an interception pass to England's Dicky Guest and they came back to 11-10. I can tell you, I was never so glad to hear a final whistle.'

Kyle dived over again in Dublin to help the Irish to a 6-0 victory over Scotland and suddenly their first Grand Slam depended on victory against Wales at Ravenhill, Belfast. 'Back in my home town as a twenty-two-year-old student, it was really something,' remembered Kyle. With the match in the balance, he put up a high kick that was dropped by the Welsh, and Irish prop Jack Daly pounced to seal the triumph. 'I can remember being carried off,' Kyle smiled, 'it was a real frenzy.' It was also Ireland's only Grand Slam to date.

Jackie Kyle

Born: 10 January 1926

Place of birth: Belfast, Northern Ireland

Caps: 52

Teams: Ireland, British Lions

LEGEND

Eric Evans

Successful Rugby Union Captain

1940s–50s Any traditional mutual disdain between lovers of football and rugby certainly did not reach Eric Evans, one of England's most successful rugby union captains. Evans trained with Manchester United's Busby Babes at Old Trafford and, himself being a qualified sports teacher, even took a few fitness sessions for Sir Matt.

In his day, as now, a front-row rugby international was not easily dismissed – after winning his first cap against the Wallabies in 1948 as a loose head prop, Evans broke his arm twice and reinvented himself as England's hooker for the 1950s. He played in the 1954 Triple-Crown-winning side and was named captain in 1956. He enjoyed his finest hour the following year when he led England to their first Grand Slam since 1928, sealing it with victory over Scotland in front of a young Queen Elizabeth at Twickenham. Evans and England were outright champions again the following year, their most impressive result being an emphatic 14-0 triumph over France.

The Busby Babes were decimated in a tragic plane crash that year and Evans retired from international rugby. He was capped thirty times during just over a decade at the top and England won nine of thirteen matches under his leadership. It was fitting tribute to the man whose biggest success was played out in front of the queen, that he was awarded the Member of the Order of the British Empire (MBE) in 1982.

Eric Evans

Born: 1 February 1921   **Died** 12 January 1991

Place of birth: Droylsden, England

Caps: 30

Teams: Old Aldwinians, Sale, England

LEGEND

Brian Bevan (LEAGUE)

Man of Mild Appearance but Supreme Rugby Gift

1940s–60s The Creator never played a finer joke than when he gave a frail, odd-looking individual by the name of Brian Bevan a supreme gift for playing rugby league. When he got off a boat from Australia at the end of the Second World War, Bevan went to Leeds and Hunslet, who took a brief look at him and showed him the door. He simply did not seem strong enough to survive a single competitive match, with bandaged knees that gave the impression his puny-looking legs were already sick.

Warrington took more time to assess him, organized a secret trial match and decided to take him on. About twenty years, 688 matches and a world-record 796 tries later, their gamble had paid off. The next-highest scorer in British rugby league, the legendary Billy Boston, 'only' got 571 tries. He said later, 'Brian Bevan is the greatest I ever played against. No one will ever get near his record, let alone beat it'. Except perhaps Bevan himself: a recent forensic check through the record books put Bevan's actual try-total, taking into account two years of semi-retirement playing for Blackpool Borough (as well as all the diverse cup matches he played), at 834 tries in 695 games. What the figures mean, whichever set you choose to accept, is that he was simply in a class of his own.

So how did he do it? With electrifying pace and one of the most elusive side-steps ever seen. He scored a hundred hat-tricks, twice managed a magnificent seven for Warrington in a single match, and won two Challenge Cups and three Championships. The only sadness was that he was reduced to playing for nationalities other than Great Britain or Australia. What a test player he would have been – that stage would probably have cemented his reputation as the deadliest try-scorer the world has ever seen.

Brian Bevan

Born: 1924   **Died**: 1991

Place of birth: Sydney, Australia

Caps: 0 (but 834 tries!)

Teams: Eastern Suburbs, Warrington, Blackpool Borough

LEGEND

Dave Valentine (LEAGUE)

World Cup Glory

1954 Dave Valentine was capped for Scotland at rugby union before winning an array of honours with Huddersfield south of the border and entertaining huge crowds in a highly talented Other Nationalities XIII.

It was with Great Britain that Valentine wrote his name in history. He played in the Ashes winning sides of 1948 and 1952 before facing the ultimate challenge in 1954. France had pushed for a World Cup because they were so short of funds. The other rugby league nations helped out and the competition was hosted by the French in October and November.

Valentine, a loose forward, was made captain when stand-off, Willie Horne, turned the honour down. No one was to be disappointed with the makeshift skipper's leadership of a squad that was missing some of Britain's best players. There were unexpected victories over Australia and New Zealand on the way to the final, where France waited with thirty thousand supporters in the Parc des Princes, Paris. The home side had twice beaten Australia in series on either side of the world in the early 1950s and everything seemed to be in their favour. However, it was the inspirational Valentine who led the Brits to a historic World Cup triumph by 16-12, and the Scotsman's last, dramatic act as an international was to lift the trophy.

Dave Valentine

Born: 12 September 1926   **Died**: 14 August 1976
Place of birth: Hawick
Caps: 2
Teams: Huddersfield, Scotland, Great Britain

LEGEND

Billy Boston (LEAGUE)

First Black Player to Tour Down Under

1950s While stationed with the army in Catterick, Billy Boston was playing rugby union with Neath when he was snapped up by league club Wigan. He scored a try on his debut and within months he was selected for Dickie Williams' Lions, as the first black player ever to be taken on a Great Britain tour down under.

His thirty-six tries made him the most prolific attacking force on that, or any other, tour. Four of those tries came in one match, the first test in Auckland, New Zealand, where no player had ever before run in so many against the Kiwis.

Boston played thirty-one times for Great Britain, scoring twenty-four tries, but his country treated him disgracefully in 1957. Returning from the World Cup Series in Australia, Alan Prescott's team stopped off to play matches in South Africa; however, Boston had been sent home alone by plane, so that his presence would not offend the apartheid regime.

For Wigan, Boston became a legend even during his career, with searing pace and powerful hand-offs his trademark. He scored 478 tries for Wigan over fifteen years and twice managed to notch up a magnificent 7 score in a single game. By the time he retired, his overall career try-count was an awesome 571.

Billy Boston

Born: 1934

Place of birth: Tiger Bay, Cardiff, Wales

Caps: 31

Teams: Neath, Wigan, Great Britain

LEGEND

Lucien Mias

'Doctor Pack'

1950s French doctor, philosopher and ferocious lock forward, Lucien Mias was as comfortable discussing the moral implications of euthanasia as he was banging the drum for a radical change in French forward play. Whatever subject 'Doctor Pack' turned his brilliant mind to, those around him tended to listen carefully. Mias became the post-war innovator whose line-out plays, combined with an emphasis on mobility and unity, added an extra dimension to the French forward armoury.

The results were stunning and by the end of the 1950s French rugby gained new respect. A hint of what was to come emerged in 1954, when France managed to earn a share of the Five Nations title. Mias's achievements as skipper in the tests against South Africa in 1958 elevated him to an entirely different plain. Michel Celaya, the tour captain, had been injured, so Mias was leading from the front when the first test got under way in Newlands, Cape Town. In a bruising encounter, the Springboks were surprised to discover that the French, previously thought of as pushovers by the Southern Hemisphere, would not give an inch. The match finished 3-3, and everything rested on the second test at altitude in Ellis Park, Johannesburg. This time it was the home side, giants of the game, who were forced into a 5-9 submission, and both Mias and his France team had won a series on their first visit to South Africa. They returned home as heroes and Mias led them to further dizzy heights, with a first outright Five Nations championship, the captain chaired-off in triumph by his grateful team-mates.

Lucien Mias

Born: 28 September 1930
Place of birth: St Germain-de-Calber
Caps: 29
Teams: Narbonne, SC Mazamétain, France

LEGEND

The Battle of Brisbane

Great Britain Win Series in Australia (LEAGUE)

1958 If any Australian tries to accuse the British of being soft, there is a simple reply: 'Battle of Brisbane, 1958'. Great Britain's rugby league victory by 25-18 in the second test on 5 July was one of the bravest performances of all time, in any sport. The British ended with only eight fit players on the pitch, because substitutions were not introduced until six years later.

Their captain, Alan Prescott, broke his right forearm after just three minutes, and played on. In the twenty-ninth minute David Bolton, the stand-off, broke his collar-bone, and was eventually forced from the pitch. Vince Karalius, a loose forward nicknamed 'Wild Bull' by the Australians, switched to fly-half and was flattened so many times he could hardly walk by the interval for a badly bruised spine. Meanwhile, Prescott had pushed a doctor away from his broken arm, telling him, 'I'll play until I drop'. Jim Challinor was one of five players taken to Brisbane General Hospital after the match with a badly bruised shoulder, as was Eric Fraser, whose elbow had ballooned to three times its normal size. England won the test when Alex Murphy combined with 'Wild Bull' Karalius for the crucial try.

Their morale sky-high, the British forgot all about a 25-8 first test defeat and thumped Australia 40-17 to clinch the series in the final test at the Sydney Cricket Ground, a record-breaking points total and margin for Great Britain against Australia. Prescott, dressed in a suit, was carried from the ground by his players, with his broken arm still in a sling, holding the trophy that symbolized his amazing Ashes triumph.

Opposite: Two years earlier, St Helens captain Alan Prescott demonstrates his physical fearlessness as he touches down his team's third try in the Challenge Cup final against Halifax in 1956.

LANDMARK

Tony O'Reilly

Record Thirty-Three Barbarians Appearances

1950s–60s

You have just turned nineteen and you walk out at Ellis Park, wearing a British Lions shirt, to be greeted by a record-breaking 95,000 screaming South Africans. Do you freeze? Not if you are Tony O'Reilly, who won his first Ireland cap while still eighteen, earlier in that unforgettable year of 1955. Instead, he ran in a vital try as the Lions beat the Springboks 23-22. O'Reilly played in all four tests, scoring again in the last match as the series was drawn 2-2.

His exploits were even more legendary when combined with the Lions' tour of Australia and New Zealand in 1959. He scored tries in the two test victories in Australia, did it again in the first and fourth tests against the All Blacks, and broke the record for tries on a Lions tour with twenty-two. That lifted his overall Lions tries total to 38 in just two tours, a record that has never been beaten.

He won twenty-eight caps for Ireland between 1955 and 1963, then another against England at Twickenham when nearing thirty-three years of age. His attacking genius helped him achieve the record thirty appearances for the Barbarians.

As if all that was not enough, when he quit rugby, O'Reilly became a billionaire businessman and was knighted. A remarkable man, Sir Anthony O'Reilly – but 95,000 South Africans had worked that out when he was still a teenager.

Tony O'Reilly

Born: 7 May 1936
Place of birth: Dublin, Ireland
Caps: 39
Teams: Leicester Tigers, London Irish, Ireland, British Lions

LEGEND

David Duckham

Born Ahead of His Time

1960s–70s Instantly recognizable by his flowing blonde hair, David Duckham swerved and side-stepped his way through opponents for 10 tries in thirty-six appearances on England's wing. It was not as spectacular a total as many flare players achieve, but when you consider that England won only eleven of those matches you begin to realize what he was up against. Duckham's swashbuckling style has led some to suggest that he was born ahead of his time, or possibly even in the wrong country, since Wales were the dominant force during his best years and England only became a truly attractive, successful team again after he had hung up his boots.

A testament to Duckham's ability to entertain was the fact that he was the only England back in the predominantly Welsh three-quarter line that inspired the Barbarians to their historic victory over the All Blacks in 1973. After his fine performance at Cardiff Arms Park, the Welsh fans christened him 'Dai' because they looked upon him as one of their own. By then, Duckham was no stranger to the unusual concept of beating the All Blacks. He had been part of the Lions' triumphant tour to New Zealand in 1971, and although the test matches were often wars, Duckham found a platform for his adventurous rugby on the islands. Encouraged to go for it by the coach, Carwyn James, Duckham ran in 11 tries in sixteen games for the Lions on that tour, more than he was able to touch down for England in his entire thirteen-year career.

David Duckham

Born: 28 June 1946

Place of birth: Coventry

Caps: 39

Teams: Coventry, England, British Lions

LEGEND

Alex Murphy (LEAGUE)

Greatest and Brainiest Scrum-Half

1960s–70s

Arguably the greatest scrum-half of all time and surely the brainiest, Alex Murphy learned how to cut it as a teenager Down Under in one of the most violent series in rugby league history. Not only did he come through the 1958 'Battle of Brisbane' in one piece, he also played a vital role in helping Great Britain clinch the series 2-1.

'I've always been a cocky little bugger,' he said later, 'but I knew I had exceptional talent and I was determined to make the most of it, which I did. Australia always had some big lads and they could do you if you let them. You had to outwit them with your brain'.

Many of Murphy's greatest international moments came surprisingly early in his stunningly successful career. Australia were the victims of his trickery in 1960, when they met in the Odsal Stadium, Bradford, to decide the World Cup. Great Britain had beaten New Zealand 23-8 and France 33-7, before disposing of the Kangaroos 10-3 in the hard-fought decider.

Two years later, Murphy was back Down Under to inspire the British to a fresh series triumph, by which time it was already becoming apparent that Murphy was unequalled. Over nineteen years he ran in 275 tries and won four Challenge Cup finals at Wembley with three different clubs. St Helens were always a good bet when Murphy was playing for them, but Leigh's opponents at Wembley, Leeds, were 5-1 on with the bookies, even with Murphy on the other side. Leigh ran riot, winning 24-7, Murphy won Man of the Match, and admitted, 'We were magnificent'. He was once asked to name the greatest rugby league player of all time, 'What, besides me?' he asked, only half joking.

Alex Murphy

Born: 22 April 1939

Place of birth: St Helens

Caps: 27

Teams: St. Helens, Leigh, Warrington, Great Britain

LEGEND

France's First Grand Slam

French Golden Era

1968 For France, the 1960s represented a golden era, when they played to their free-flowing strengths, further developed their rugby identity and fought a series of running battles with Wales for Five Nations domination. In 1968 they went one step further than winning the tournament, and pulled off their first ever Grand Slam. They were led by a dynamic, six-foot flanker called Christian Carrere, a tough man from Tarbes in the Pyrenees, now more famous for tennis tournaments.

Tries by the wingers, André Campaes and Bernard Duprat saw off Scotland 8-6 at Murrayfield. And Campaes went over again when France beat Ireland quite comfortably by 16-6 at the Stade Colombes, with Benoit Douga the other try-scorer, Pierre Villepreux the supplier of a precious 7 points with his goal-kicking, and Jean Gachassin successful with a drop-goal attempt.

England were expected to provide more formidable opposition in the same arena, but it did not turn out that way. While the boot of Bob Hiller kept the visitors in some kind of touch, Gachassin ran in a try and the half-back pairing of Lilian and Guy Camberabero kicked 8 points between them. Lilian's drop-goal was accompanied by another from Claude Lacaze and stilted England were soon out of it.

That set up a perfect finalé against Wales in Cardiff, and the home side looked to have the upper hand when they led 9-3 at half-time. The French stormed back with tries from Lilian Camberabero and the captain, Carrere, while Guy Camberabero kicked a full set with a conversion, penalty and drop-goal. The Welsh were beaten 14-9, the French had done it, and the 'Tricolores' were Grand Slam champions.

Opposite: Captain Christian Carrere is chaired off the pitch by his jubilant team-mates after their final win that secured France's first Five Nations Grand Slam.

LANDMARK

No-Hopers Dare to Dream

Great Britain Win Ashes Down Under (LEAGUE)

1970 Aged thirty-one, Frank Myler was widely regarded as the Great Britain captain charged with taking a bunch of no-hopers to Australia for an Ashes series that would heap humiliation on the founders of the game. When they lost the first test in Brisbane, few back home saw any reason to change their minds and braced themselves for the inevitable. However, emerging stars, like Mal Reilly and Roger Millward, were learning fast in a new environment, and by the time the second test in Sydney came around Millward, in particular, was ready to shine. He pierced the Kangaroos' line for 2 tries and added no fewer than 2 goals, thus equalling Lewis Jones' 20-point haul in Brisbane back in 1954, a total achieved in slightly less spectacular style with 10 goals.

When Great Britain maintained their momentum to take the third and final test 21-17 in Sydney just a fortnight later, Myler lifted the Ashes as though an impossible dream had come true. The true enormity of the success emerged only over the following decades, when British teams tried and failed to repeat the feat. Those 1970 Lions were the last to win the Ashes in Australia, and the last to register successive victories against the Kangaroos in the same year.

A few months later, Great Britain made it three-in-a-row with an 11-4 win at Headingley during the World Cup, but it was what they had done in the back yard of the strongest rugby league nation in the world that would set Myler's Miracle Men apart from those who followed.

Opposite: Great Britain continued their run of success right up to the World Cup final at Headingley – here Australia's Mark Harris is brought down by Jim Thompson – but Australia were to retain possession of the Cup that year.

LANDMARK

Unbullied by All Blacks

Lions Beat All Blacks in Series

1971 John Dawes' British Lions won a test series in New Zealand for the first time because they refused to be bullied by Colin Meads' fearsome All Blacks.

Ian 'Mighty Mouse' McLoughlin scavenged a priceless try off a charge-down as the Lions won a dour first test in Dunedin 9-3, but the backlash came in the form of a heavy second test defeat.

Before the third test in Wellington, the Lions' coach, Carwyn James, and his captain, fellow Welshman Dawes, did a superb job of repairing the Lions' self-belief. There were two other Welshmen at half-back who did not need lessons in confidence, whatever the hammering they had already taken. Legend has it that Barry John, the fly-half, said, 'Just give me the ball and I'll win it for you. It's only the All Blacks'. With the help of a hand-off like a battering ram, his deceptively powerful scrum-half, Gareth Edwards, did just that, and John's try meant he had kept his promise. Gerald Davies had already gone over and the Lions had won 13-3.

In the all-important fourth and final test, the lead changed hands several times, but a huge drop-goal from J.P.R. Williams ultimately earned the Lions a series-clinching draw. When his kick went over J.P.R. waved at the crowd like a pop star, which was exactly how the history-makers were received when they arrived home.

Opposite: The victorious 1971 British Lions team returning home as stars. In front are captain John Dawes (left), manager Dr Doug Smith (centre) and Barry John (right).

LANDMARK

Mike Gibson

Versatile, Dependable Star

1960s–70s

Mike Gibson is remembered for his dependability, longevity and versatility as a star for Ireland and the British Lions. He was not built powerfully, yet he was reliable in defence, as all good centres have to be. Between 1964 and 1979, he won sixty-nine caps for Ireland, a record total at the time for any International Board nation, and beaten only recently by a fellow Irishman in 2005, when the lock Malcolm Kelly won his seventieth cap against Scotland. In Gibson's era, far fewer internationals were played and, incredibly, he was thirty-six when he played his last match for his country against Australia in 1976. No wonder his record lasted for twenty-six years.

A modest man and a coach's dream, Gibson could slot in anywhere if an Irish three-quarter line's circumstances demanded it, and he played in four different positions during his test career. Although he only scored 9 tries, that statistic does not do justice to the frequency with which his clever breaks set up scores for team-mates. He still managed 115 test points, partly due to 16 penalties, 7 conversions and 6 drop-goals. With exquisite handling and deft footwork, Gibson was an automatic selection for Lions tours Down Under in 1966, to South Africa in 1968 and to New Zealand in 1971. He made history of a quirky kind when he came on as international rugby's first ever replacement during a test in Pretoria between the Lions and South Africa.

He will be best remembered for his reliability under intense pressure and his brave creativity in the greatest Lions tour of them all, the 1971 series win against the All Blacks. There, with the rest of John Dawes' team, he wrote his name in rugby legend.

Mike Gibson

Born: 3 December 1942

Place of birth: Dublin, Ireland

Caps: 81 (69 for Ireland, 12 for Lions)

Teams: Ireland, British Lions

LEGEND

Barry John

The King

1960s–70s

There is no player in the history of rugby whose name conjures up quite the sense of awe that accompanies the words 'Barry John'. The New Zealanders thought he must have come from another planet in 1971, because he simply did not look powerful enough to cause their muscular team so much trouble. His elusive running, superb decision-making, unshakable confidence and devilish kicking turned the series around from fly-half. It was not only the way he made a fool of New Zealand full-back Fergie McCormick with his teasing first-test kicks, or the sublime try he scored in the third test at Wellington, but also the near-panic he caused in New Zealand with his casual flare, as he nonchalantly notched up 30 of the 48 points the Lions scored in the series. He became known as 'The King'.

John was lucky, of course, because he was paired at half-back for Wales and the Lions with another player who could have claimed, had it been in his character to do so, to be the greatest rugby player the world had ever seen. Gareth Edwards and Barry John developed an understanding that gave their God-given talent a perfect launch pad. The results were explosive, the entertainment immense and no one wanted it to end. It did though, and much sooner than anyone had anticipated. While Edwards used to counteract the pressures of being a rugby god with humour and a spot of fishing, John found it harder, despite his confident exterior. He retired at twenty-seven, having played just twenty-five times for Wales. Like George Best, his equivalent in football, he found the fame more unnerving than the sporting opposition.

Barry John

Born: 6 January 1945

Place of birth: Cefneithin, Wales

Caps: 30

Teams: Wales, British Lions

LEGEND

Roger Millward (LEAGUE)

Blanking out Pain

1970s One of the best players ever to wear a Great Britain shirt, Roger Millward first won international honours as a teenager when he played against France in March 1966. The following year, when he was still only twenty, he scored a hat-trick of tries for his beloved Hull Kingston Rovers against the touring Australians, in a dramatic 27-15 victory.

After finishing the season as top scorer with 38 tries, Millward was picked for Great Britain's World Cup squad. On the 1970 tour to Australia he scored two hat-tricks for his country and the most points in a match between Great Britain and Australia, 20, in the second test in Sydney. He came closest to World Cup glory while captaining England for seven out of eight matches in 1975. Millward was outstanding in the draw in Brisbane, and again when England beat the Kangaroos in Wigan. But a defeat against Wales ultimately cost the English the trophy.

Millward played in three World Cups, made forty-seven international appearances (twenty-nine of them test matches) and ran in 20 tries. He was even more prolific for Hull Kingston Rovers, for whom he scored 207 tries in 406 matches. More than 600 goals pushed his total points tally up to a staggering 1,825 and in one match against Hunslet he managed to score 31 points.

His last high point was perhaps his most memorable of all, in the 1980 Challenge Cup final against city rivals Hull. Millward broke his jaw after fifteen minutes, played on and had it knocked back into place by another crunching tackle. He was still blanking out the pain when he lifted the cup.

Roger Millward

Born: c.1947

Place of birth: Castleford

Caps: 29

Teams: Castleford, Hull KR, Cronulla Sharks, Great Britain

LEGEND

Gareth Edwards

Barbarian Magic – The Greatest Try

1973 It was, quite simply, the try of the twentieth century. That title was never seriously disputed, even in a sport that produces so many thrills and spectacular scores.

To reach the try-line against any All Blacks side takes guile, but what the Barbarians did at Cardiff Arms Park on 27 January 1973 was so audacious, so fluent, and so miraculously successful that it will be celebrated for as long as the game of rugby union exists.

The magical move began with no fewer than three stunning side-steps from Phil Bennett, the Welsh fly-half. Seemingly trapped near his own try-line, yet refusing to kick for safety, Bennett brought roars from the crowd with his matador skills before off-loading to J.P.R. Williams. Anyone who believes the opposition were a passive support act in a harmless exhibition match should recall that All Blacks three-quarter Bryan Williams tried to take his namesake's head off at this point. Yet the move kept flowing down the left, the momentum maintained by superb exchanges between John Dawes, Tom David and Derek Quinnell. Finally, from nowhere, Gareth Edwards appeared with an electrifying burst of pace and dived over to round off the stuff of dreams. Was Quinnell's final pass a fraction forward? Who cares?

Gareth Edwards

Born: 12 July 1947

Place of birth: Gwaen-ace-Gurwen

Caps: 63

Teams: Wales, British Lions, Barbarians

LEGEND

One of Best Ever Union Teams

The Lions Win Series in South Africa

1974 Due to the thuggery that gave the tour lasting infamy, it is easy to forget that Willie John McBride's 1974 British Lions were one of the best teams ever to have played rugby union. To go unbeaten in South Africa was a truly remarkable achievement. The Lions had lost three and drawn one in their last two test series there, in 1962 and 1968. The ability to play superb, flowing rugby in South Africa was usually the preserve of the South Africans. Yet even before the Battle of Port Elizabeth, which will be covered elsewhere, the Lions had established their superiority over the Springboks.

The first test in Cape Town was a hard-fought affair, with the tourists coming out on top by 12-3; but the second test in Pretoria was as rampant a display as had been seen by a visiting team in a test match. The Lions romped home 28-9, despite physical provocation, and it was hard to doubt their superiority. What happened in the third test, with J.P.R. Williams running half the length of the pitch to throw a punch, was scarcely believable.

The Lions' destructive behaviour in their Port Elizabeth hotel was equally lamentable by modern standards, though perhaps more in keeping with the extremes of a booze-driven rugby culture at the time. Lost somewhere among the negative headlines was the result of the match, another thrashing for South Africa by 26-9. To outclass the Springboks once was extraordinary; to do it twice was historic. With the series won, the 13-13 draw in Johannesburg was little more than an afterthought. McBride's Lions were already all-time greats who should not be remembered simply for the fighting.

'I believe there is a great secret in life. It is realizing when to work, and when to play. Those 1974 Lions knew it and that was most important. ... I knew I could rely on them when I needed them to be at their best.'

Willie John McBride (pictured opposite acknowledging the cheers of the waiting crowds at Heathrow)

LANDMARK

J.P.R. Williams

The Complete Player

1970s There have been more elegant runners and prolific goal-kickers operating from his position on a rugby field, but there has never been a greater full-back than John Peter Rhys Williams. Ferocious in the tackle, immense under a high-ball, J.P.R. was a man who lived for the physical challenge and seemed determined to show that he was as hard as any forward. His long hair and dramatic sideburns could not disguise an iron will, and when Willie John McBride called 'ninety-nine' on the infamous tour of the 'Invincible' Lions to South Africa in 1974, Williams ran half the pitch to thump the Springbok lock, Johannes van Heerden, a man almost twice his size.

When J.P.R., a surgeon by day, had his cheek ripped apart by the studs of an All Blacks prop called John Ashworth, he still had the composure to dish out advice to team-mates before leaving the pitch to supervise the repair job.

He won three Grand Slams with Wales, helping to secure the 1976 triumph with a tackle on Jean-François Gourdon that knocked the French winger clean off his feet and yards off the pitch. Though his running style was not the prettiest, J.P.R. was just as big a threat in attack, as 5 tries in ten tests against England showed. They never beat him.

He was not a regular international goal-kicker, but that did not mean he was no good at it. He let fly with a towering drop-goal against the All Blacks on the 1971 Lions tour, and punched the air in triumph when it sailed over, because he knew he had effectively clinched the series. J.P.R. was that rare commodity – the complete player.

J.P.R. Williams

Born: 2 March 1949

Place of birth: Cardiff, Wales

Caps: 63 (55 for Wales, 8 for British Lions)

Teams: Wales, British Lions, Bridgend, London Welsh.

LEGEND

Willie John McBride

Ninety-Nine

1974 Willie John McBride will be forever associated with a special number – ninety-nine. It is the number that symbolizes the refusal of the 1974 British Lions to be bullied and beaten into submission by the Springboks, a process the Lions felt had been allowed by their referees for too long, and lay behind their superb home record. Whether there was any truth in the allegation hardly seems to matter now. 'Ninety-nine' was the call during the third test in Port Elizabeth, and when McBride's players heard it, they knew it was the order to attack their closest South-African-Test opponent. It was dirty and outrageous, and it worked.

The Lions won their first series in South Africa 3-0, with one test drawn. For McBride it was the highlight of five Lions tours and seventeen tests for the tourists, an all-time record. He had been part of the glorious series win in New Zealand three years earlier, but even that paled into insignificance.

McBride retired from the international arena the following year, with sixty-three caps for Ireland, twelve as captain. His last fifty-two appearances for his country had come without interruption, but he later insisted, 'Nothing I ever did on a rugby field comes close to '74'.

Of his infamous tactic in South Africa, this is what he said: 'There was method to the madness. You see, there were fights breaking out all over the place ... the ninety-nine call ensured that everyone had a chance to settle their differences and be ready to play thirty seconds later. Even a South African referee, so I reasoned, couldn't send all fifteen of us off.' He was right. With no video evidence available, they all got away with it. They would not be so lucky in the modern era.

Willie John McBride

Born: 6 June 1940

Place of birth: Toombridge, County Antrim, N. Ireland

Caps: 80

Teams: Ireland, British Lions

LEGEND

Andy Irvine

Thrilling Running

1970s The proud nation of Scotland has come up with many a gutsy, defiant team, but fewer individual players who could take the breath away with their running skills. Andy Irvine was therefore a rare specimen, a full-back who could conjure for Scotland, and occasionally the British Lions, something of what Serge Blanco produced in such style for the French. Not the safest defensive technician the game has ever seen, he was still the man his team-mates most wanted to see in possession when the Scots were about to launch a counter-attack.

His distinctive, skipping stride, his swerve, balance and grace made him a formidable weapon when the conditions were right for running. If his handling sometimes let him down, it seemed only to add to the sense of theatre. Irvine played the game the way it was meant to be played – sprinting with his knees high and his limbs a whirlwind until he reached the try-line or found support.

Few British three-quarters quite conveyed the same love of running, or thrilled Murrayfield crowds quite like Irvine, an unusually spontaneous British rugby entertainer.

Andy Irvine

Born: 16 October 1951

Place of birth: Edinburgh, Scotland

Caps: 60

Teams: Scotland, British Lions

LEGEND

Bill Beaumont

Plain 'Bill' to Many

1970s–80s

William Blackledge Beaumont played international rugby for seven years. Not the longest stay at the top among the game's great legends, but in that time he won such affection from the English public that he later built a career as a lovable television personality. The proud Lancastrian lock captained his country twenty-one times and earned thirty-four international caps, at that time a record for someone playing in his position. In 1975 he made his debut against Ireland in Dublin and two years later he was a late call-up for the British Lions' tour to New Zealand, playing the last three tests.

Beaumont was made captain of England in 1978 for the game against France in Paris, and also led the North of England to victory over the All Blacks in 1979. Yet his greatest achievements came in 1980, when he inspired a mediocre England side to their first Grand Slam for twenty-three years, and their first clear Five Nations championship for seventeen years. The clincher was a tense 9-8 win over a Wales team that had scored 2 tries to 0 and were down to fourteen men, but it did not matter. Beaumont was chaired-off in triumph, and soon set his sights on leading the Lions in South Africa, the first English captain to do so since Douglas Prentice in 1930. Unfortunately, the Lions lost the first three test matches against the Springboks. At least they ended on a high, though, with tries from Andy Irvine and John O'Driscoll securing victory in the fourth test in Pretoria. Ever popular, Beaumont played fifteen times for the Barbarians before retiring due to injury in 1982.

Bill Beaumont

Born: 9 March 1952

Place of birth: Preston, Lancashire

Caps: 41

Teams: England, British Lions

LEGEND

The Rise of The Oaks

Romania Beat France, Wales and Scotland

1980s The rise of Romania in the 1980s is a stunning success story with a poignant ending. The Oaks, as they are known, were not previously a respected force in world rugby, and the Home Nations began to award international caps when they played Romania only from 1983. Perhaps they saw what was coming. Romania had beaten France convincingly in Bucharest by 15-0 in 1980. They repeated the feat again in 1982. Then it was the turn of Wales to travel to rugby's new cauldron. They lost by an embarrassing 24-6 thanks to a second-half onslaught by the home side. Romania's flanker Florica Murariu, a tough army officer, was a try-scorer that day: he had played a part in all the shocks so far and was about to be part of one more. Scotland went to Bucharest the following year and when they led 16-9 at half-time, it looked as though they had avoided making the obvious mistake of underestimating their opponents. However, the Romanians, with Murariu typically rampant in their pack, produced a historic comeback to win 28-22.

By the time Romania went to Wales in 1988, Murariu, now a veteran at thirty-three, was captain. He led his country out in Cardiff and stunned his hosts with a 15-9 victory that made the world take notice. The following year, the world had another reason to take notice of Romania, when the country's dictator, Nicolae Ceausescu, was overthrown in a pre-Christmas revolution. In the chaos, Murariu, the military man and rugby legend with thirty caps for his country, was shot dead at a road block.

Opposite: The Romania team years later in 1998, still on the world stage.

LANDMARK

Jonathan Davies

The Last Great Welsh Fly-Half

1980s–90s Jonathan Davies has been described as the last great Wales fly-half, a man whose flare followed in the rich tradition of Barry John and Phil Bennett. When Davies decided to defect to rugby league in 1988, it marked the peak of union's hostility to the rival code. He had inspired Wales to the Triple Crown that very year, dazzling England with his unpredictable runs and sinking Scotland with crucial drop-goals.

Then three things happened to make Davies consider his future. His son, Scott, was born, so money became more important. Wales were battered by 50-point margins in New Zealand, despite Davies sprinting the length of the field to score in the second test, and he felt his suggestions for improvement were ignored. Finally, there was a mini-disaster at home to Romania, when the Welsh wizard did not play his best game and was stunned to be criticized publicly by Wales's management.

So, when rugby league club Widnes came calling, he jumped ship, switched codes and moved north, playing for Great Britain, Wales, Widnes, Warrington and even the Australian side Canterbury Bull Dogs during an impressive career. He went back to union in his final years, to complete a total of thirty-seven caps, but not before other top Welsh union players had followed him into rugby league. These events rocked rugby union to the core and pushed the amateur code another few steps towards professionalism.

Jonathan Davies

Born: 24 October 1962

Place of birth: Trimsaran, Carmarthenshire

Caps: 32

Teams: Neath, Llanelli, Widnes, Warrington, Cardiff, Wales

LEGEND

Serge Blanco

Smoking Genius

1980s How could a man never comfortable unless he had a Gaulloise cigarette hanging from his mouth produce such magical rugby every time he kicked his habit for long enough to play a match? It is one of the enduring mysteries of the game, perhaps even of medical and sports science, that Serge Blanco, who smoked sixty cigarettes a day, seemed to have more puff than opponents who were dedicated fitness fanatics. It says everything about his natural ability and rubbery, elusive running that he still became one of the game's greats, despite his persistent habit.

When Blanco was given the ball, he was capable of doing anything when he was into his long, loping stride. His counter-attacks were legendary and it was considered rugby suicide to kick a ball anywhere near him. Opponents still did it.

The Biarritz flyer's devil-may-care approach captured the essence of everything that is so beautifully unpredictable about French rugby. Greater tacklers have played test rugby at full-back (J.P.R. Williams of Wales to name just one), but Blanco was a supreme entertainer with grace to match. When he wasn't smoking.

Serge Blanco

Born: 31 August 1958

Place of birth: Caracas, Venezuela

Caps: 93

Teams: France, Biarritz Olympique

LEGEND

Ellery Hanley (LEAGUE)

The Black Pearl – Mr Magic

1990 Arguably the finest player the sport has ever seen, no defence could stop Mr Magic from opening his box of tricks. Most top rugby league players would be regarded as legends if they achieved a try-scoring rate of one every other game. 'The Black Pearl' scored an amazing 440 tries in 539 first-class matches in Britain and Australia. His adoring fans were therefore confident they would see him score almost every time, whether he was playing on the wing, at stand-off, in the centre or even at loose-forward.

In the 1984–85 season, he scored 55 tries in only thirty-seven games, the first man to ground more than 50 since Billy Boston. He commanded a world record £150,000 transfer fee when he moved from Bradford to Wigan. At international level, he became a huge star when he ran in 12 tries during the 1984 Lions tour to Australia. He was made Great Britain captain in 1987, and the following year led his country to their first win over the Kangaroos for ten years. Hanley's 8 tries in that series brought the British agonizingly close to regaining the Ashes. He was awarded the Golden Boot in 1989, rugby league's way of telling him that he was without equal.

He said later, 'I wanted to be the best player in the world and it was something I strove for, so this was the biggest honour of my career'. That year he also scored one of the best tries the game has seen as he helped destroy St Helens 27-0 at Wembley. When Hanley became British coach for the 1994 Ashes, he was the first black man to reach such a post in any team sport.

Ellery Hanley

Born: 1961

Place of birth: Leeds

Caps: 34

Teams: Bradford Northern, Wigan, Balmain, Western Suburbs, Leeds, Great Britain

LEGEND

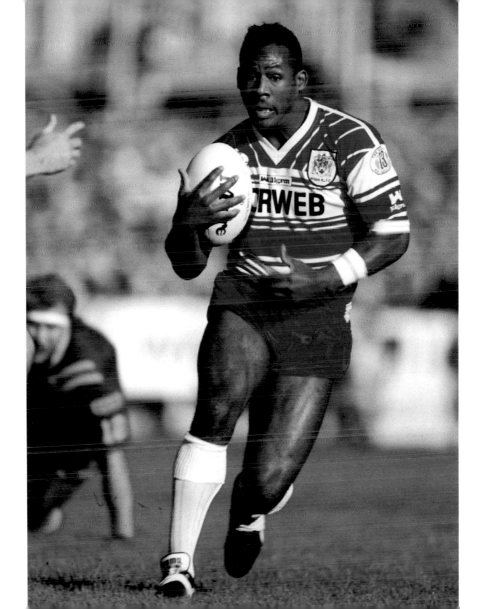

Sole's Scottish Brave-Hearts

Scotland 13 England 7

1990 Every so often, a player refuses to bow to the inevitable, and demands the sort of defiance from his team-mates that changes the course of sporting history. In 1990, David Sole, captain of Scotland, was one such man. While the rugby world was writing off their chances of giving Will Carling's all-powerful England a decent match, other ideas were taking shape north of the border.

Scotland had enjoyed a good Five Nations themselves, and if they achieved mission impossible and beat England at Murrayfield, they would be crowned Grand Slam champions instead of Carling's highly-fancied favourites. Walking, or rather marching, out to battle proved to be the key. Sole's simple but brilliant idea was a fearsome declaration of intent. Carling, England's captain, was vulnerable to bold psychological warfare, and Sole must have sensed it. The pace of that dramatic entrance evoked the spirit of down-trodden Scottish armies from centuries gone by, as they prepared for a bloodbath against the Auld Enemy.

It looked so intense, and provoked such a fierce roar from the Murrayfield crowd, that the stage was set for one of the biggest shocks in Five-Nations history. Sure enough, Sole's Scottish brave-hearts emerged from battle as 13-7 winners thanks to Tony Stanger's late try.

David Sole (pictured opposite, centre)

Born: 8 May 1962

Place of birth: Aylesbury, England

Caps: 47

Teams: Bath, Edinburgh Academicals, Scotland, British Lions

Motivating England After Murrayfield

Will Carling's Back-to-Back Grand Slams

1991–92 England's captain, Will Carling, used the sickening shock of 1990 to motivate his players for the next two Grand Slams, inviting them to remember how they felt at Murrayfield in order to ensure that it never happened again. The ploy worked a treat and gave England a ruthlessness, at a domestic level at least, to go with their abundance of ability.

Carling's era, which began with an explosive win over Australia at Twickenham in 1988, made rugby union popular and cool again in England. Young, good-looking, charming and a winner, he projected the sort of image that was in keeping with a steady move towards professionalism. There were faults, of course, and Carling found criticism hard to handle. He was accused of arrogance and overconfidence, and on the world stage these weaknesses, sometimes projected on to the England team as a whole, were exploited by Australasian rivals to bring them crashing down.

Due to the World Cup disappointments of 1991 and 1995, it is easy to forget that the England team did fulfil its true potential in the Five Nations, as it was called then, with back-to-back Grand Slams in 1991 and 1992 – the first time this had been achieved by an England team since 1923 and 1924. There were nervous moments over those two years, such as during the 21-19 win over France at Twickenham in 1991, when Philippe St André's try completed a counter-attack that swept the length of the pitch, but Carling's England had effective runners of their own in Jeremy Guscott and Rory Underwood. Above all, they had the crushing power of men like Dean Richards and Brian Moore up front to keep the ship steady, plus the goal-kicking of Rob Andrew. One way or another, England did it, and deservedly so given all their other heartbreaks.

'Murrayfield was the big turning point for me as a captain. I realized we had to be more ruthless and professional in our approach to these games. '

Will Carling

Rory Underwood

The Flying Winger

1990s Rory Underwood was known as The Flying Winger because he was a Royal Air Force pilot with a passion for speed. He flew some of the quickest machines in the world in his day job and sometimes seemed to be moving just as fast when he sprinted down England's wing. A major star in Will Carling's England team, he won eighty-four England caps, a record until passed by Jason Leonard. Underwood was a deadly finisher and scored a record 49 international tries. His scampering style was not necessarily one for the purists, but he ate up the ground at a frightening pace on his way to the try-line. His cold efficiency, even when space was tight, proved a match-winner in the glamorous Carling era, and he also won six caps for the British Lions, touring Australia in 1989 and New Zealand in 1993.

When his brother Tony joined him as a test winger, they were the first family double act to play for England since 1937. Like Tony, Rory was not considered to be the safest defender and his handling sometimes left a little to be desired. Underwood hated the limelight and preferred to get on with the business of being a rugby international as quietly as possible. His mother, of Chinese extraction, was the flamboyant member of the family, cheering wildly when both her sons played for England together. There were no World Cups to celebrate, but back-to-back England Grand Slams in 1990-91 and twelve years at the top were still a huge achievement.

Rory Underwood

Born: 19 June 1963

Place of birth: Middlesbrough

Caps: 90

Teams: Leicester Tigers, Bedford, England, British Lions

LEGEND

Martin Offiah (LEAGUE)

Chariots

1990s Martin Offiah's try-scoring spree was so devastating that it evoked memories of Brian Bevan, the Australian-born Warrington star, who ran in some 796 tries over twenty years, mostly in the 1940s and 1950s. Coming as it did in the modern era, Offiah's milestone – he ran in his 500th try in a 37-14 victory over London – was perhaps even more impressive, with defences supposedly built of men with even stronger physiques. He scored 181 tries for Wigan in 144 games, and enjoyed a similar success rate after his £440,000 record transfer to Wigan, where he touched down 186 tries in 158 appearances. In 1992, he even scored 10 tries in a single match, and when you throw in a goal, and 3 drop goals, for good measure, his Wigan tally came to 749 points. Some said he did not have quite the rugby brain of Alex Murphy or even Ellery Hanley, but if you could not catch him it hardly seemed to matter.

In the 1994 Challenge Cup final he left the entire Leeds team for dead as he raced from one end of the pitch to another for one of the greatest tries of all time. Not bad for a man dismissed as 'a clown' by the St Helens board when Murphy recommended they bring him north. In that same year he won the World Club Challenge with Wigan, seeing off Australia's best, Brisbane Broncos, and there was never any doubt that the player nicknamed 'Chariots' (after the film *Chariots of Fire*) could make his extraordinary talents work for him on the international stage. He scored 26 tries in thirty-three matches for Great Britain, a fantastic record. Endearingly, Offiah never forgot his rugby union roots with Rosslyn Park in London, and said recently, 'I still get excited by both union and league'.

Martin Offiah

Born: 29 December 1966

Place of birth: Essex

Caps: 33

Teams: Rosslyn Park, Widnes, Wigan, London Broncos, Salford, Great Britain

LEGEND

Gavin Hastings

Skilled and Determined

1980s–90s Everyone knew Gavin Hastings was going to be special when he kicked 6 penalties on his Scotland debut in 1986 to pip France 18-17 at Murrayfield. Against England at Murrayfield, 21 points led a 33-6 rout that provided the momentum for a share of the Five Nations championship. Hastings' Rugby World Cup adventures began with 27 points against Romania in 1987 and, after also starring in the 1991 and 1995 tournaments, he became cumulative points record-holder with 227.

The powerful full-back was not captain the day Scotland secured their 1990 Grand Slam against England, but he played a crucial role in Tony Stanger's decisive try. When he was made Lions captain for the tour to New Zealand ahead of Will Carling in 1993, many an eyebrow was raised. However, despite losing the series 2-1 to the All Blacks, Hastings' ability to remain cool under fire increased his stature. He also showed what a steely nerve he had developed when it came to kicking under pressure, and boosted his overall points total for the Lions in test matches to a record 66.

Perhaps his finest hour was, as we shall see shortly, his contribution to Scotland's historic victory over France in 1995. He retired from international rugby later that year with a record 733 points for his country (667 in test matches), having won sixty-one caps. It was a deeply impressive achievement for a player not blessed with lightning pace, but with enough weight, skill and determination to make his mark when the posts or try-line were in his sights.

Gavin Hastings

Born: 3 January 1962

Place of birth: Edinburgh, Scotland

Caps: 61

Teams: Watsonians, Cambridge University Rugby Football Club, Scotland, British and Irish Lions

LEGEND

Scotland Win in France

Jinx Broken

1995 Grainy images of Jim Telfer skipping through the French back in 1969 were all the Scottish had by which to remember good times in France. They had endured twelve successive defeats in Paris and their captain, Gavin Hastings, had been around for too many of them. Before the match, he made it clear that he meant Telfer no disrespect, but he would rather be watching Scottish victories in Paris on a video of better quality. By the end of an epic afternoon in the old Parc des Princes, Hastings and fly-half Gregor Townsend had together created a high-quality sporting drama in glorious modern technicolour, the images as clear and joyful as any Scot could wish for.

It was Townsend who scored Scotland's first try and when Hastings converted and added two penalties, the bagpipes were starting to herald a 13-5 half-time score-line.

However, with their wonderful running skills, the French can never be written off. Back they stormed, despite another Hastings penalty, and by the closing stages the home side had taken the lead through 2 tries from their captain, Phillipe Saint-André, and another by Jean-Luc Sadourny.

Then, just as Scotland was bracing itself for another Parisian tale of woe, Hastings took a pass from Townsend only moments from full-time, and burst the French line to dive in under the posts. A simple conversion confirmed it: Hastings had 18 points, Scotland had broken their miserable jinx, and Telfer's heroics were finally consigned to the film library.

Opposite: Gavin Hastings bursts through the French defences to score a try in the dramatic match against France in February 1995.

All Change!

Union Turns Professional, League Switches to Summer

1995–96 In 1995, after the commercial success of the Rugby World Cup in South Africa, the union game bowed to the inevitable and finally went professional. Almost to the last, traditionalists tried to resist the march of time and claimed that rugby union would be destroyed by greed. The hypocrisy and deceit in the sport had been getting ridiculous, with many players already receiving payments in roundabout ways. A new era dawned and at last Europe's top players could be paid in line with what some of their Southern Hemisphere counterparts were rumoured to have been receiving for a while.

So far, the fears of rugby's amateur-loving doom merchants have proved largely unfounded. The international game, in particular, has gone from strength to strength, with each World Cup bigger than the last.

The instant success of professional rugby was also a factor in the switch of British rugby league to a summer schedule in 1996, with the season lasting from February until September. This had more to do with the lucrative contract offered to the RFL by BSkyB and Rupert Murdoch's desire to win a power struggle with the Australian Rugby League. As with union, the league game has adapted well to new conditions.

The two codes have survived and thrived since 1995 and 1996, the years when rugby said, 'All Change!'

Opposite: Former international Rugby Union players Robert Norster (left), Richard Moon and Peter Winterbottom (right) help launch the Rugby Union Players Association in London after the association is formed to assist players in the light of the new professional regulations brought in by the IRB.

LANDMARK

Adventurous Outlook with Nothing To Lose

British Lions Win Tour of South Africa

1997 Even though this was the first professional Lions tour, coach Ian McGeechan and captain Martin Johnson knew they would be up against it. Having won the World Cup in 1995, South Africa had taken their eye off the ball the following year, and lost a series in their own back yard to New Zealand for the first time. The idea of another series defeat in front of their fans was unthinkable.

The Lions, on the other hand, played as though they had nothing to lose, adopting their trademark adventurous approach. Matt Dawson, their scrum-half, threw an outrageous dummy in the first test at Cape Town for a match-winning score as red pockets of Lions fans roared their approval. The English contingent, who had seen their team destroyed by the All Blacks in the same Newlands arena two years earlier, were particularly satisfied with the surprising 25-16 victory.

The Springboks stormed back to make it harder in the second test, and in the dying minutes the series rested on a drop-goal attempt under extreme pressure by Jeremy Guscott, much better known for his snaking runs than any ability with the boot. Guscott's effort sailed through the posts, the Lions had clinched the match 18-15 and the series with a test to spare. Predictably, South Africa took revenge in the final test, but it was too late. Johnson's heroes came home triumphant.

'The fastest prop I've ever seen!'

Jeremy Guscott on Scott Gibbs

LANDMARK

World Cup Semi-Final

France Beat All Blacks 45-31

1999 Some World Cup matches are so dramatic that they overshadow the final itself, and are remembered for far longer. Such a game came around in 1999, in the form of a semi-final that the All Blacks were firmly expected to win against the puzzlingly inconsistent French. After all, the 1990s' most exciting side could not keep blowing their chances on the World Cup stage ... could they?

By the end of a scintillating afternoon at Twickenham, the All Blacks' dream had, indeed, bitten the dust yet again. Furthermore, in the immediate aftermath of one of the greatest displays of all time, New Zealand were no longer the most exciting rugby runners in the world – France had taken over. Those who witnessed the action will never forget it. Jaws dropped, breaths became hard to take, and heads shook in sheer admiration for the French comeback.

Jonah Lomu looked to have destroyed the French with two monstrous solo tries, just as he had crushed England at this stage four years earlier. However, 'Titou' Lamaison, who liked his red wine as much as his rugby, had other ideas – having already opened France's try-scoring following a blistering run from Christian Dominici, Lamaison now pinged over drop-goals and penalties to keep his side in touch. Then France's killer three-try burst began. Dominici touched down thanks to Fabien Galthié's perception, Lamaison conjured a magical cross-kick for Richard Dourthe to catch and score, and then Lamaison again released Olivier Magne for Philippe Bernat-Salles to complete the rout. It was mind-blowing.

'People back home were baying for my blood.

They have got it.'

John Hart on announcing his retirement as New Zealand coach following the back-to-back losses to France and South Africa

Opening Victory Secures Welcome

Italy Win Six-Nations Opener

2000 On 5 February 2000 an Italian dream that had been years in the making finally came true in Rome's packed Stadio Flaminio. The Romans claim to have invented rugby in 388 AD, calling their version Harpastum. The trouble was that in the modern era, no one wanted to let their descendants play in Europe's biggest tournament, despite three successive World Cup appearances by the Italians. Season after season, quiet negotiations behind the scenes brought the barriers gently down. Now, finally, Italy were not just taking part in the new Six Nations, they were actually beating the previous year's champions.

By the time Italy's substitute, Giampiero De Carli, rammed his way across the line from close range, the Six Nations' new boys were home and dry. They had beaten Scotland 34-20, when any half-respectable result would have sufficed as an introduction. Diego Dominguez had kicked 29 points, though Italy coach and former All Black Brad Johnstone reminded him that it was the others who had put the little maestro in so many scoring positions.

This was the start Italy had craved. There would be plenty of Six Nations set-backs ahead, as they tried to find consistency in the regular company of far more experienced rugby nations, but the nature of that opening victory bought Italy the time and patience that was needed. They had arrived and they remained welcome.

'I'm very pleased now. The importance of rugby has been shown to Italy.'

Coach Brad Johnstone on the benefits of Italy joining the tournament

LANDMARK

Diego Dominguez

The Little Magician

1990s–2000s One player stood head and shoulders above the rest when Italy burst on to the international scene at the World Cups of 1991, 1995 and 1999. The fact that Diego Dominguez stood only five feet seven inches tall and remained one of the shortest players in the squad did not matter. The fly-half's stature lay in his imperious kicking and superb decision-making. Argentina must have wondered how they let their former understudy to the legendary Hugo Porta slip through their fingers.

Instantly likeable, quiet and engaging, Dominguez nevertheless had a ruthless streak as he put top teams to the sword. Rugby is a team game, but if any one man launched his adopted country, Italy, into the Six Nations, it was Dominguez. He celebrated by slotting six penalties from all angles, three drop-goals of alternating height and power, and one immensely difficult conversion from the right-hand touchline to clock up a personal tally of 29 points in Italy's inaugural Six Nations victory over Scotland by 34-20. Dominguez retired at the end of that season, but was brought back because he was deemed irreplaceable. He won his seventy-fourth and final cap against Ireland in February 2003, when he was almost thirty-seven.

Diego Dominguez

Born: 25 April 1966

Place of birth: Córdoba, Argentina

Caps: 74 (Italy)

Teams: Italy, Argentina

LEGEND

Jason Robinson

Mr Twinkle Toes – Billy Whizz

1990s–2000s It is doubtful whether any runner in rugby league or union has ever made his legs pump so fast as Mr Twinkle Toes, the magician better known as Billy Whizz.

Robinson won twelve Great Britain caps and played 302 rugby league games, scoring 182 tries. He was a self-confessed bad-boy until former All Black Inga Tuigamala showed him the path towards Christianity. Billy Whizz became calmer inside but his ability to shred defences remained undiminished. Robinson eventually switched to rugby union and a glittering career with Sale Sharks after playing part of a season with Bath.

On the international stage, he scored 19 tries for England in just thirty-three internationals, including his country's only try in the 2003 World Cup final triumph. The following autumn Robinson became the first mixed-race and former rugby league player to captain England, celebrating with a hat-trick of tries in a thumping win over Canada. He had represented the British Lions as far back as 2001, scoring tries in the first and last tests of a highly entertaining series against Australia. However, he was stifled in the 2005 series in New Zealand and retired from international rugby later that year. Some believe he could yet make a comeback for World Cup 2007.

Jason Robinson

Born: 30 July 1974

Place of birth: Leeds, England

Caps: 19 (League), 44 (Union)

Teams (League): Wigan, Great Britain, England

Teams (Union): Sale Sharks, Bath, England, British and Irish Lions

LEGEND

Jason Leonard

'The Fun Bus'

2003 When England won the World Cup in 2003, one man on that pitch in Sydney knew that his career had come full circle at last. Having made his debut against Argentina in 1990, a young Leonard was thrust into the cauldron of the 1991 World Cup, tasting narrow and bitter defeat to the Australians at Twickenham. Twelve years later, the boot was very much on the other foot and the Australians were getting to know heartbreak in their own back yard.

Leonard had been sent to lend extra stability to England's pack as the pressure mounted in the closing stages of the 2003 final. His contribution was not spectacular, but he had never been one for fireworks on the pitch. Leonard was the prop who got on with his highly influential work while others stole the headlines, until one day the world looked around, and there he was, the most capped international of all time, with 119 caps, five of which came in tests for the British Lions.

It was not long before Sean Gregan of Australia surpassed that total, but Leonard did not mind. He had more than enough memories by then, such as back-to-back Grand Slams with Will Carling's England in 1991 and 1992. At the time, he did not think much of it, even though no England side had done it since 1923 and 1924. As Leonard explained later, 'It was only when we fell short again during the next two seasons that I realized just how hard it had been to achieve what we did in those two Grand Slam years'. That was about as near to self-congratulation as you would hear from Jason Leonard, one of the most popular players the game has ever known.

Jason Leonard

Born: 14 August 1968

Place of birth: Barking, England

Caps: 119

Teams: Saracens, Harlequins, England, British and
Irish Lions

LEGEND

The Best in The World

England Win Rugby World Cup

2003 England were the best in the world in 2003 and no one seriously doubted it, but by the time the World Cup arrived late in the year they were slowly running out of steam. Martin Johnson's team forced their way to the final with an unconvincing 28-17 victory over Wales in the quarter-final, and a dour 24-7 win over disinterested France in the semi-final. A big bonus was that Australia pulled off an upset in the other semi-final by knocking out the highly fancied All Blacks. However, there was nothing in England's recent form to suggest that World Cup glory would come easily against the hosts.

There were nearly 83,000 people in Sydney's Telstra Stadium and the English who had travelled across the world were stunned by Lote Tuquiri's opener for Australia. The inspirational Johnson rallied his troops and Lawrence Dallaglio's break allowed Jonny Wilkinson to release Jason Robinson. He sizzled on a try-scoring burst to the corner.

England were sitting pretty at 14-5 when half-time came, but the Wallabies fought their way back into it after the break. The nagging accuracy of Elton Flatley brought the game back to 14-14 and forced extra time. The goal-kickers, Wilkinson and Flatley, landed one more apiece but sudden death was looming. Twenty-one seconds before the end of extra time, a storming run from Matt Dawson set up Wilkinson's legendary drop-goal and England, at 20-17, had become the first European side to win the World Cup. Almost a million people celebrated their return with the Webb Ellis Trophy in London's West End.

'A hot chocolate please...'
Jonny Wilkinson ordering room service at
England's team hotel after his drop-goal won
England the World Cup, while the rest of his
team-mates drowned themselves in champagne

LANDMARK

Martin Johnson

A Colossus of A Captain

2003 Under Johnson, England had all the gritty leadership it needed to at last mount a successful World Cup campaign. When Johnson lifted the trophy in 2003, those who knew him best said they had never seen an expression of such wild, primitive triumph on his rock-hard face before.

The Leicester lock had known glory in Europe with his club, and plenty of winning days in Will Carling's talented England team, but when it came to the World Cup crunch, there had only been heartbreak.

Johnson, whose girlfriend at the time was a New Zealander, had to deal with unwanted media intrusion prior to the 1995 World Cup semi-final against the All Blacks. Jonah Lomu's single-handed destruction of England in Cape Town put paid to all that.

England flattered to deceive again in 1999, but under Johnson's captaincy in 2003 it was clear that there was to be no more failure. It was always said that the England team that year was packed with captains and, in a way, it was true; but none of them had Johnson's presence or steely determination to turn those long-held World Cup dreams into reality. When the margin between victory and defeat in the final against Australia was wafer-thin, it was Johnson's strength of character that made the difference.

Martin Johnson

Born: 9 March 1970

Place of birth: Solihull, West Midlands

Caps: 84

Teams: Leicester Tigers, British and Irish Lions

LEGEND

Jonny Wilkinson

Passion for Goal-Kicking

2003 England's quiet fly-half will for ever be remembered for a glorious night in Sydney in November 2003. With the World Cup hopes of an entire nation hanging by a thread, Wilkinson steadied himself for a drop-goal under heavy pressure. Unusually for such a perfectionist, he did not strike the ball quite right, but it sailed willingly through the posts just the same. There was no time for Australia to come back and England won the World Cup, the first European team to do so.

While his team-mates celebrated long and hard around Circular Key, Wilkinson returned relatively early to the squad's hotel on Manley Beach. As thousands of England supporters packed the pubs and clubs of central Sydney for a champagne party that would last until the sun came up, Wilkinson retreated to the peace of his hotel room and ordered a hot chocolate.

The Newcastle stand-off had always harboured an obsessive passion for goal-kicking, and for a while he became the best in the world at his art. Children and fellow professionals alike began to copy his distinctive preparation, with hands clasped together in front of a gently leaning torso. Sadly, however, Wilkinson's dream night in Sydney was followed by one injury after another, and it was feared he would never hit similar heights again.

Jonny Wilkinson

Born: 25 May 1979
Place of birth: Frimley, Surrey
Caps: 52
Teams: Newcastle Falcons, England

LEGEND

Sir Clive Woodward

A Winning Formula

2003 After the 1999 World Cup failure, Woodward, meticulous and moody in equal turns, survived calls for his head, with former England captain Will Carling among his fiercest critics.

What a difference four years made. Woodward, a graceful England centre in his day, went away to put things right and came back with a glorious winning formula. All areas of England's preparation for World Cup 2003 were impeccable and nothing was left to chance. Even before the tournament, England's record against the biggest countries showed that Woodward had built a team of world-beaters. His players' needs were met to the finest detail.

Neither Woodward nor his team seemed to care that they went into the World Cup as favourites who might have peaked a fraction early. When their dominance was challenged by stubborn Australia in that memorable final, Woodward had instilled enough confidence and composure in his side to cope with the crisis.

Central London was packed with almost a million people for the home-coming parade. However, even before a disastrous tour of New Zealand with the British Lions, Woodward – knighted and known as Sir Clive – had shocked the game by announcing his intention to switch to soccer coaching.

Sir Clive Woodward

Born: 6 January 1956

Place of birth: Ely, Cambridgeshire

Caps: 23

Teams: Harlequins, Leicester Tigers, England, British and Irish Lions

LEGEND

Brian O'Driscoll

Maturity and Flare

2000s Brian O'Driscoll is widely regarded as one of the finest centres Ireland – or indeed Europe – has ever produced. His flare made the world sit up and take notice in the late 1990s but he soon added maturity to his armoury and took over as Ireland captain when Keith Woods stepped down in 2003.

In 2005, O'Driscoll was given the honour of captaining the British and Irish Lions on their tour to New Zealand. Controversy still rages about what happened to end O'Driscoll's series in the very first test. All Blacks Tana Umaga and Keven Mealamu combined to execute a highly dangerous 'spear tackle', dumping O'Driscoll down head-first so that he sustained a badly dislocated shoulder. The New Zealanders claimed it was an accident, and O'Driscoll accepted their apology at face value, but there can be little doubt that the Lions captain had been targeted as a major threat to the All Blacks, who went on to win the series comfortably.

O'Driscoll was back at the top of his game in 2006, leading Ireland to the Triple Crown Trophy and only narrowly losing out to France for the Six Nations. O'Driscoll was voted Player of the Tournament.

Brian O'Driscoll

Born: 21 January 1979
Place of birth: Clontarf, Dublin, Ireland
Caps: 65
Teams: Blackrock College RFC, Leinster, Ireland, British and Irish Lions

LEGEND

Wales Win Grand Slam

Brief Flashback to The Golden Era

2005 Wales secured their first Grand Slam for twenty-eight years through sheer force of will. They were roared on by 74,000 fans in the stadium, at least another 100,000 nearby, men and women who had flooded into the pubs of Cardiff especially and anyone who had loved the nation's golden era of the 1960s–70s. Not even the Irish could deny it was Wales's turn, since the men in green had stopped the home side from gaining a single victory against them in Cardiff since 1983.

Tries from the irrepressible prop, Gareth Jenkins, and the skilful full-back, Kevin Morgan, assured the Welsh the party they had been waiting for all those years. After a 32-20 victory over the Irish, Gareth Thomas and Michael Owen lifted the Six Nations Trophy together as a signal for the celebrations to begin in earnest.

There was a sense that it might be the Year of the Dragon when Gavin Henson's mighty penalty defeated England 11-9 in the opener at the Millennium Stadium, a moment that lifted Henson to celebrity status almost instantly. Then came a thrashing of Italy, a glorious comeback in the 24-18 win over France, and the destruction of Scotland 46-22 at Murrayfield, where 40,000 Welsh fans claimed to be present.

After the Grand Slam was secured, the winning coach, Mike Ruddock, said, 'The team drew strength from the hard times they had been through together'. Every Welsh rugby fan in the world could have said the same.

'It was an unbelievable atmosphere in the stadium, the support was tremendous.'

Wales wing Shane Williams

Brian Carney (LEAGUE)

First Irishman to Play for Great Britain Since 1957

2000s Brian Carney is no ordinary rugby league player. In 2003 he became the first Irishman to play for Great Britain since Tom McKinney back in 1957. The winger's inclusion in the Super League Dream Team that year said everything about his quality, and he is now regarded as one of the finest wingers in the world.

Born in Cork, Carney started out playing Gaelic Football before setting his sights on rugby league. He moved to Wigan Warriors in 2000 and has never looked back since, catching the eye of the Australians in his first year in the international arena. Having proved himself against the best in Britain, Carney craved a new challenge, and there was no greater test than to pit his skills against the stars of the NRL (National Rugby League) in Australia. He got his chance when his British club understood his dreams and gave him the freedom to negotiate a contract with Newcastle Knights in the NRL.

However, in 2006, Carney summoned all his skills to play against the Australians in the Tri-Nations, and although he had to come off injured, he contributed to the shock 23-12 Great Britain win in the tournament's first match between the countries.

From Gaelic Football to stardom with Great Britain, to a life of sunshine, spear-fishing and top rugby in Australia, Carney has lived life to the full.

Brian Carney

Born: 23 July 1976

Place of birth: Cork, Ireland

Caps: 3

Teams: Newcastle Knights, Gateshead Thunder/Hull FC, Wigan Warriors, Gold Coast, Ireland, Great Britain

LEGEND

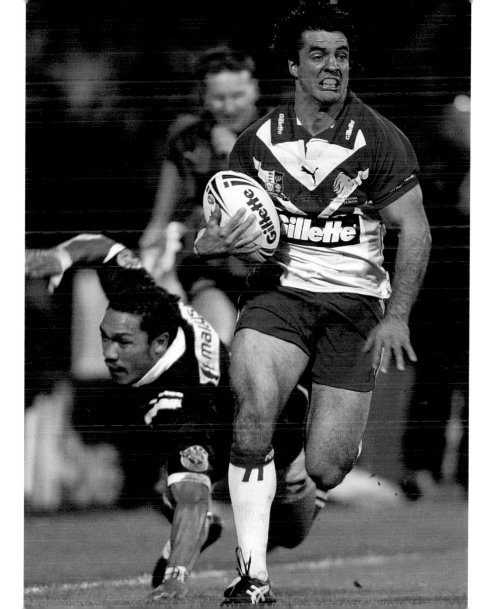

Jamie Peacock (LEAGUE)

One of The Finest Forwards in the World

2006 Great Britain captain for the Tri-Nations tournaments in 2005 and 2006, Jamie Peacock is widely regarded as one of the finest forwards in the world. He made his Super League debut for Bradford in 1999 and learned his trade quickly. By 2000 he was helping the Bulls to their Challenge Cup success over Leeds at Murrayfield, and soon the honours were coming thick and fast.

Apart from thriving in Grand Finals and Challenge Cup finals, he has also tasted glory in the World Club Challenge, when he was part of the Bulls side that overcame the mighty Newcastle Knights of Australia.

An uncompromising prop, Peacock soon won the respect of his peers, and was voted Players' Player of the Year in 2002, as well as Man of Steel for making such an impact on the game.

By then he had already become a Great Britain international and enjoyed the ideal start in a debut against the Australians at Huddersfield, and he scored a try as the British beat the Kangaroos. It was not the last time he would savour victory against the most feared side in the world, leading England to a storming triumph early in the 2006 Tri-Nations.

Jamie Peacock

Born: 14 December 1977

Place of birth: Leeds, West Yorkshire

Caps: 14

Teams: Stanningley ARLFC, Leeds Rhinos, Bradford Bulls, Featherstone Rovers, University of Wollongong, England, Great Britain

LEGEND

The Rise of Georgia

The Story So Far

2003–07

Towards the end of 2006, Georgia drew 11-11 against Portugal in Lisbon, thereby achieving qualification for their second successive Rugby World Cup. It is a remarkable feat, given that Georgia has managed, so far, to mark out just eight rugby pitches for a grand total of three hundred adult players. With some 65,000 present at Tblisi's national stadium for a European Nations Cup match against Russia, it seems that the potential for rugby to become a major sport in Georgia is huge.

The team, known as the Lelos after an old Georgian game that bears similarities to rugby, has come a long way since players first began to adapt Russian-made tractors so that they could have their own cut-price scrum machines. At the centre of the story are the coach Claude Saurel, who packs most of his players off to the lower leagues in France to learn the basics, and the country's most distinguished player, the full-back, Paliko Jimsheladze. In 2006, Jimsheladze was honoured before the game in Tbilisi against the Barbarians, in which he won his fiftieth cap, the first Georgian to do so.

It was Jimsheladze who lent respectability to Georgia's first World Cup in Australia, with eleven points for the unknowns against the giants of South Africa, who won 46-19. There was another encouraging score-line against Uruguay, 24-12, although Georgia still finished as losers.

Having beaten Portugal over two matches, with Jimsheladze scoring 7 points in the 17-3 first-leg victory, Georgia prepared for their second World Cup adventure, this time in France, where they would play the hosts as well as Argentina and Ireland. Georgia's story is only just beginning.

Opposite: Georgia's players celebrate after their World Cup qualifying match against Portugal, November 2005.

AFRICA

They say that sport and politics do not mix, but try telling that to South Africa. Since the Springboks have always been the continent's dominant rugby force, much of Africa's rugby history has been played out against a political backdrop: ugly when that backdrop was apartheid, inspirational when it was Nelson Mandela, who used rugby to help unite his 'rainbow nation' in 1995.

It is worth considering the extent to which sporting principles may have been compromised in the pursuit of political gain during South Africa's rugby lifetime, even in the idealistic fervour of that World Cup final in Johannesburg. What we should not forget is the way in which generations of wonderful players have tried to express themselves, some more distracted by off-field events than others. Meanwhile, supporting African nations have offered shocks and tragedies of their own. The continent is addictive, and its rugby story is no exception.

The Green Jersey Adopted

South Africa's First Series Win Against British Tourists

1903 South Africa's amazing story of test success began in 1903, after a twenty-year apprenticeship. Canon George Ogilvie, headmaster of the Diocesian College in Cape Town, was the founding father of rugby in the region and had set up the Western Province Rugby Football Union back in 1883. The first British touring team arrived in 1891 and only conceded one try in twenty matches. Significantly, they presented the Currie Cup for the first time, to Griqualand West for the best performance from a province on the tour.

In 1896 Barry Heatlie borrowed the myrtle green shirts of the Old Diocesian club, in the hope of boosting morale during a tough series against the British. The jerseys brought South Africa luck at last when, having lost the first three tests, the home side won the last match to show just how much they had learned from the opposition.

Heatlie was still around to captain South Africa for the 1903 series against the British, and decided to adopt the same green jerseys as he went in search of a similar result. The first match was drawn 10-10 at the Wanderers club in Johannesburg, and the deadlock continued at Kimberley where there was no score. Cape Town was different, however, and South Africa won 8-0 at Newlands to secure their first series triumph. A big forward, Alex 'Oupa' Reid, used his strength to score one try, and the winger, Joe Barry, sprinted over for the other. Healtie's boot rounded off the scoring, and from that day the famous green jerseys were adopted on a permanent basis. They continued to work like a charm. South Africa did not lose another series, home or away, until 1956!

Opposite: The reign of the green jersey continues. Here South Africa celebrate winning the Dubai Rugby Sevens trophy in December 2006.

LANDMARK

Tour of Britain

First Use of Springbok Nickname and Logo

1906–07

It is nothing new for touring teams to feel pressurized by the media. Indeed South Africa's nickname, the Springboks, was born of the timeless tension between players and press as far back as 1906. The South Africans had sailed up to play the Home Nations and journalists wanted a nice catchy name for them when they arrived. The captain, Paul Roos, realized that if he did not come up with something quickly, the media would choose a name themselves. Roos and his management team sat down and came up with 'De Springbokken'. *The Daily Mail* in London called them the Springboks and the identity was created. Players were soon wearing blazers with a springbok motif stitched into the left breast pocket.

On the pitch there were mixed fortunes. The tourists lost 6-0 to Scotland at Hampden Park, but came bouncing back against Ireland in Belfast. The Springboks were 12-3 ahead at half-time and, despite an Irish comeback, finished 15-12 victors. The hero of the day was Johannes Albertus Loubser (Bob to his friends), who ran in 2 tries on the wing. 'Japie' Krige and Anton Stegmann scored the others as the Springbok three-quarters stretched their legs.

A trip to Swansea to play Wales brought another successful day. Bob Loubser, Steve Joubert and 'Klondyke' Raaff all scored tries in a relatively comfortable 11-0 victory. That left England as the last opposition in Britain, and the Springboks fought hard to earn their share of a 3-3 draw. The buoyant tourists crossed the Channel to play a France XV, although ironically the French Test team had sailed in the opposite direction. The South Africans put a makeshift French side to the sword by 55-6. The Springboks were up and running as a touring rugby force.

Opposite: The South African squad in 1906 on their tour of Great Britain, with captain Paul Roos (centre of middle row) and Bob Loubser (far left of middle row).

LANDMARK

Controversy on Maiden Tour

Springboks' First Tour of New Zealand

1921 Not for the last time, the South Africans caused great controversy on this maiden tour to New Zealand because of their attitude to race relations. The flashpoint came when the Springboks played a Maori team at Napier and won 9-8. The local paper ran a report from a South African correspondent, who could not have been more provocative if he had tried. The article about the game read, 'This was the most unfortunate match ever played. Only great pressure brought to bear on the manager (HC Bennett) induced the Springboks to meet the Maoris, who had assisted largely in the entertainment of the Springboks. It was bad enough having to play a team officially designated 'New Zealand Natives' but the spectacle of Europeans frantically cheering on a band of coloured men to defeat members of their own race was too much for the Springboks, who were frankly disgusted.' A Maori doctor, Te Rangi Hiroa, protested about the tourists and wrote '...we stand appalled at the bad taste and ignorance displayed'.

New Zealand beat the Springboks 13-5 at Dunedin, but the South Africans, captained by 'Boy' Morkel (who was actually thirty-six) hit back in Auckland. Billy Senden scored the important try as the Springboks won 9-5.

The final test ended 0-0, mainly because the rain was so torrential that the mud-covered players could barely distinguish one team from another and spectators slid down the Western Bank as the earth turned to treacherous mud. The series was drawn, as was a dividing line in attitudes to skin colour.

Opposite: Maoris undaunted. The New Zealand Maori team perform their Haka several years later, in 1926.

LANDMARK

Danie Craven

Player and Coach

1930s–50s In many ways Danie Craven *was* South African Rugby in the twentieth century, at least the best part of it. He made his debut for the Springboks against Wales in 1931 at twenty-one, and played a striking role in their 8-3 victory in Swansea. Over the next seven years, he became one of the greatest scrum-halves the world has ever known. Although he never got to play against England or France as a number nine, he faced the British Lions, Australia and New Zealand, and his seven-year test record reads like one long success story.

There was the 3-2 series triumph over an excellent Wallabies team in 1933 and a further 2-0 series win in their own back yard in 1937. That same year, he was part of a Springboks side that came from behind, having lost the first test in Wellington, to take the series in New Zealand 2-1. His last test in 1938 was a defeat to the British Lions at Newlands, but the Springboks had already wrapped up the series with two victories. World War II robbed him of more glorious moments and after sixteen tests and 3 tries his playing career was over.

Craven was appointed Springboks' coach in 1949 and won his first ten matches, including four straight victories over New Zealand during their tour of South Africa. The Springboks played twenty-three matches under Craven and won seventeen, making him one of the most successful coaches his country has ever had.

Craven was Executive President of the South African Rugby Football Union when he died in 1993. How he would have loved his country's World Cup triumph of 1995.

Danie Craven

Born: 11 October 1910   **Died**: 4 January 1993

Place of birth: Lindley, South Africa

Caps: 16

Teams: Eastern Province, Western Province, South Africa, Northern Transvaal

LEGEND

Hennie Muller

The Greyhound

1950s Great sportsmen vary in their manner of preparation for big occasions. For some, a few minutes in the dressing room to focus on the task ahead is more than enough. Hennie Muller, on the other hand, once admitted that he stopped talking to his wife three days before a test match. This happened on sixteen occasions between 1949 and 1953, although the silence was sometimes aided by the fact that he was in another part of the world for the build-up to a vital game.

As a number eight, Muller was simply electrifying. His Afrikaans nickname 'Windhond' means greyhound. Hennie could run like the wind, kick with either foot, handle like a dream and tackle too. He was one of the fastest back-rows the game had known, a complete player.

The Scots discovered that to their cost when they walked into the Murrayfield Massacre of 1951, a 44-0 thrashing which saw Muller cross for one of 9 tries scored by the Springboks. The shell-shocked Scots carried Muller off in triumph, showing more sportsmanship than defensive know-how on the day. The other Home Nations were not so easily beaten, with Ireland losing 17-5, Wales defeated 3-0 and England succumbing 8-3. Muller kicked a penalty and a conversion to make the difference in that last one, and took his side to France knowing they were one game away from a glorious Grand Slam. An emphatic 25-3 victory secured the Greyhound's place in history, and he scored one of the 6 South African tries. He began his last series against Australia, won 3-1, with a try in the opening exchanges at Ellis Park.

It is not known whether Muller's long-suffering wife was pleased when he retired or not.

Hennie Muller

Born: 26 March 1922   **Died**: 26 April 1977
Place of birth: Witbank, South Africa
Caps: 13
Teams: South Africa

LEGEND

Tom Van Vollenhoven

Union's Loss and League's Gain

1950s–60s When a flying Springbok winger called Tom Van Vollenhoven scored a hat-trick against the British Lions in 1955, word got back to two rugby league clubs, St Helens and Wigan, in the north of England. By 1957, Saints had outmanoeuvred their rivals and evaded the furious South African Rugby Union to spirit their future superstar away to his new professional home. The speed, side-step and swerve that were features of the Van Vollenhoven game helped him adapt to a very different kind of rugby challenge. In the 1958–59 season alone, 'Vol' sizzled over the line for 62 tries. He was joined at St Helens in 1959 by fellow South African Jan Prinsloo and for a while they occupied a wing each.

By 1968 'Vol' had scored 392 tries in 408 appearances for Saints, and there was a fierce debate among league fans over who was the greatest finisher, the powerful Billy Boston or the supremely pacey Tom Van Vollenhoven. A Calypso record cut to coincide with his testimonial insisted that the South African was 'The Greatest of them All.'

As with that eye-catching rugby union performance of 1955, he had a habit of running in hat-tricks or scintillating masterpieces on the big occasion. Even with a pulled hamstring, he managed a hat-trick against Hunslet in the 1959 Championship final. He scored a further 3 tries in his very last club appearance against Wigan at Knowsley Road. Ageing or injured, he was still better than the rest.

From a glittering career, Van Vollenhoven left more than one try for connoisseurs to savour, including a ninety-yard dash in the 1961 Challenge Cup final, featuring inter-passing with team-mate Ken Large and a devastating finish. Union's loss was very definitely League's gain.

Tom Van Vollenhoven

Born: 29 April 1935
Place of birth: Bethlehem, South Africa
Caps: 7
Teams: Northern Transvaal, St Helens, South Africa

LEGEND

Craven's Revenge

False Start of Rugby League in South Africa

1957 Danie Craven would have his revenge for the loss of Tom Van Vollenhoven to rugby league – on a plate and in the same year of 1957. Having already played in a gruelling World Cup, held in Australia and won by the host nation, the players of Great Britain and France were taken to play exhibition matches in South Africa. The idea was to make rugby league popular there and give test-playing nations another lucrative destination. The impact that such a foothold might have on the game of rugby union in South Africa was not at the forefront of the rugby league administrators' thoughts.

Craven, still furious about the Van Vollenhoven affair and perhaps fearful of more defections, prevented the first rugby league exhibition match from being played in Johannesburg, and packed the teams off to the outpost of Benoni, sixty miles away. Naturally, the crowds were thin and there was another problem – the French were not interested. They had sustained enough bumps and bruises at the World Cup and were not keen to put their bodies on the line yet again. They trained twice a day to keep fit but when it came to the first match they did not seem to try. The one-sided contest looked ridiculous and the farce was repeated in Durban.

The English, who were not training but at least took the matches half-seriously, thumped their opponents yet again. Before the third scheduled match in East London, the rugby league promoters had realized that there would be no foothold for their sport in South Africa, not that year, anyway.

Opposite: Rugby union retains prominence over league in South Africa. The South African rugby union team back in 1952 with Danie Craven on far right.

LANDMARK

Frik du Preez

Player of the Century

1960s There cannot be many greater tributes than to be named 'Player of the Century' by the fans of the country. This was the honour bestowed upon Frik du Preez of South Africa, and it was a measure of his popularity that he won the accolade even though his ten-year career took in one of the bleakest periods in the Springboks' long test history.

In 1965, having gone down to France the previous year, they won just one test match out of six, including two defeats to Australia and a 3-1 series loss in New Zealand. Despite this, the reputation of du Preez among the supporters clearly remained unblemished. He threw body and soul into each and every game he played for South Africa, showing pace, kicking ability, handling skills and, above all, grit.

Du Preez started out in Test rugby as a flanker, converting the only try of the game in the Springboks' 5-0 win over England in 1961. Two penalties followed in a 12-5 victory over Scotland, but du Preez soon switched to lock and his kicking duties were curtailed.

He is best remembered for a stunning forty-yard dash in Pretoria, his hair waving in the wind as he flew down the touchline. Before the British Lions could recover from the line-out chaos from which he had emerged, du Preez had reached the try-line for a vital score. That 25-20 victory was a key moment in the 3-1 series triumph over the 1968 Lions, and du Preez ended his thirty-eight-test career with a third straight victory in the 1971 series against Australia. In good times or bad, he was a joy to watch.

Frik du Preez (pictured tackling a Southern Counties player in 1960)

Place of birth: Rustenburg, South Africa

Born: 28 November 1935

Caps: 38

Teams: Northern Transvaal, South Africa

LEGEND

More Work Required in Defence

South Africa lose series 3-0 to Great Britain (LEAGUE)

1962 Behind-the-scenes political wrangling did not necessarily help South African rugby league grow healthy roots; even so, the team that took on Great Britain in three matches in 1962 certainly managed to put some points on the board.

The National Rugby League (NRL) and Rugby League South Africa (RLSA) were two separate organizations set up to oversee the growth of the game at league level. The NRL brought over Wakefield Trinity to test the quality of a South Africa Combined XIII, which was found wanting in a 59-3 defeat. The RLSA set about arranging for Great Britain to visit South Africa, but not before ex-Warrington, Easts and Australian coach Dave Brown had knocked the South Africans into shape.

Even Brown's skills could not work miracles in the short time available, but some highly entertaining rugby was played. The British won the first match 49-30, the second by a far narrower margin, 39-33, and the third 45-23, the biggest win of the lot.

To concede 133 points in three matches showed that more tactical work was required in South Africa's defence, though there was clearly nothing wrong with their basic skills in attack. The British insisted their hosts should not be downhearted, though the political differences between the twin administrations was still a problem.

Opposite: Wakefield Trinity, the team that tested the South Africa Combined XIII, celebrating another victory in 1962, against Huddersfield.

LANDMARK

Death Knell for Rugby League in South Africa

Tour to Australia and New Zealand

1963 It was not so much the results of the test matches in Australia that knocked the wind out of South African rugby league (although they were bad enough); far more damaging were the number of defeats the tourists sustained against the country's revered club sides.

Everyone knew how much was riding on the tour's ability to show that a Springbok rugby league team could hold its own in international company. Even the Australians wanted it to succeed, so that they could have new, strong opposition to play on a regular basis. They offered the tourists sixty-five per cent of gross gate receipts or a guaranteed minimum of 45,000 Australian dollars. All was going to plan when South Africa beat North New South Wales and Monaro in early matches. Experienced professionals, such as Fred Griffiths, Oupa Coetzer, Alan Skene and Col Greenwood, had qualified to represent South Africa and, initially, their know-how appeared to be paying off. Doubts crept in when South Africa lost the next seven matches, and were crushed 49-5 by Sydney a week before the first test. The international opener went no better and Australia won 34-6, with Johnny Raper the scourge of the tourists.

South Africa's luck seemed to have changed at the start of the second test when they scored within seconds, but then came an avalanche 54-21 defeat. Not even a 4-3 test victory in New Zealand could turn the tide of opinion and South African rugby league was doomed for a few more decades.

Opposite: Even with the help of experienced professionals such as Oupa Coetzer, South African rugby league just would not take off. Here, Coetzer, playing for Wakefield Trinity, moves in to tackle Wigan's Eric Ashton as Ashton lays the ball back to teammate Billy Boston in 1963.

LANDMARK

Controversial Tour of Australia

Anti-Apartheid Demonstrations Dominate

1971 South Africa won the series 3-0 but it was not remembered for the rugby. Anti-apartheid protestors dominated from start to finish, even forcing a state of emergency to be declared in Queensland, where the test match was switched from Brisbane's Ballymore Stadium to the Exhibition Ground because it was easier to defend. Two-metre-high barbed wire fences were erected to keep the angry crowds away from the players.

While demonstrators tried to saw down goalposts in Sydney, a five-thousand-strong crowd marched on Olympic Park in Melbourne for a confrontation with mounted police armed with truncheons. There were 140 arrests in Melbourne alone, 700 during the entire tour.

Hotels and airlines began to cancel Springbok reservations and the tourists had to be increasingly secretive in their movements. One player said, 'It's like playing James Bond twenty-four hours a day. Our matches only last eighty minutes – how could our cricketers do five days at a time?' He was right about the cricketers. South Africa's tour to Australia later that year was cancelled as people-power won the day. It was a triumph for the protestors, who had put mixed-race couples in the Springbok hotels to show them how the free world lived. Increased justice for the Aboriginal people of Australia also became a burning issue. Meanwhile, South Africa grew a little more isolated.

Opposite: A girl is carried into a police van after trying to disrupt the game between the Springboks and a New South Wales team on 10 July 1971. South Africa won that game 25-3.

LANDMARK

Morne du Plessis

An Outstanding Record

1970s Few captains have a better track record in test rugby than Morne du Plessis, a six-foot-five-inch number eight whose imposing frame suppressed needless dissent. He inspired unity and confidence in team-mates, doubt in the opposition. At line-outs he became king, almost untouchable. In a ten-year test career, du Plessis played twenty-two matches, winning eighteen. He led the Springboks in thirteen tests and lost only twice.

As an introduction to the international arena, circumstances could not have been tougher than during the 1971 tour to Australia, when the Springboks were targeted by protestors because of the anti-apartheid regime back home. Du Plessis showed the resilience required to survive Down Under, but received a rugby lesson from the British Lions in 1974, temporarily at the cost of his place in the team. Victories over France restored his confidence, and he was made captain for their visit to South Africa, which resulted in two more Springbok wins. All this acted as preparation for the severe examination of his leadership credentials which would come when New Zealand toured in 1976. The Boks took the first two tests but lost the third, setting up a cliffhanger of a climax to the series. South Africa edged the decider 15-14 and du Plessis carved his name in history.

A convincing series win over the 1980 British Lions helped put old ghosts to rest, and there was one more glittering swansong still to come. When South Africa won the World Cup in 1995, du Plessis was their manager. 'We won because we put the right family together,' he said. 'A sports team is a family.' His was always a happy one.

Morne du Plessis

Born: 21 October 1949

Place of birth: Krugersdorp, South Africa

Caps: 22

Teams: South Africa

LEGEND

David Barends (LEAGUE)

South Africa's Missed Opportunity

1970s Seven years after South African rugby league died a rather forlorn death in Australasia, one of the country's most talented youngsters, David Barends, packed his bags and left for Britain. He knew that even if the sport did make a miraculous recovery in his homeland, he would not be allowed to take part in it. The reason was that Barends was a black man, and therefore his talent, and that of many like him, were considered irrelevant, no matter how grave the crisis in the game.

Barends travelled to northern England, where he carved out a wonderful career in rugby league, with Wakefield Trinity, York, Bradford and then Great Britain. He was among his side's try-scorers in the 1977–78 season's Premiership Final victory over Widnes by an emphatic 17-8. In April 1979, he was captured on camera literally jumping over a Wakefield defender to deposit the ball beyond the try-line while upside down, his legs almost vertical in the air (pictured opposite). It was a fitting symbol for the way in which he had made a mockery of the prejudices of apartheid, finding a platform for his skills, and enjoying every minute regardless.

Barends was picked for the Great Britain tour of Australia and New Zealand in 1979. The test matches in Australia were lost but nearly all the other games won. The British managed to win the series in New Zealand, with the only loss being the final test match.

In 2000, Barends returned to Cape Town to receive the Honour of Yesterday's Heroes award for black stars discriminated against during the apartheid years.

David Barends

Born: 31 October 1947

Place of birth: Elim, Cape Province, South Africa

Caps: 2 (Great Britain)

Teams: Wakefield Trinity, York, Bradford Northern, Featherstone Rovers, Other Nationalities, Great Britain

LEGEND

Naas Botha

Nasty Booter

1980s Naas Botha introduced his awesome kicking skills to the world with a touchline conversion to sink the British Lions in the third test in 1980, a kick that won the match 12-10 and gave the Springboks an unassailable 3-0 lead in the four-game series. The legend of 'Nasty Booter' had been born.

He did not run further than he had to, not when he could release team-mates or call upon a magical boot to do the hard work for him. In twenty-eight test matches, the South Africa fly-half scored only 2 tries, yet he dropped 18 goals and kicked 312 points, a record at the time. Had South Africa been part of the international community for a larger part of Botha's career (which stretched from 1980 to 1992) and had it been the custom to play as many test matches then as we see now in world rugby, it is unlikely that Percy Montgomery (the latest Springbok record holder) would have beaten Botha's projected total.

Botha was extraordinarily prolific, averaging more than 10 test points in every match he played. For Northern Transvaal's 'Blue Bulls' he once dropped 5 goals in a match against Natal, and in total managed to amass 2,511 points. South Africa's hero has the rare distinction of knowing that a rose was named after him – Rosa Naas Botha. He also has the satisfaction of knowing that he owned some of the finest kicking boots the world has ever seen.

Naas Botha

Born: 27 February 1958

Place of birth: Breyten,Transvaal

Caps: 28

Teams: South Africa, Northern Transvaal

LEGEND

Errol Tobias

First Black Springbok Starter

1981 On 30 May 1981, a thirty-one-year-old black man, who still was not allowed to vote, represented South Africa in a test match against Ireland at Newlands, Cape Town. The match was won 23-15 but the inclusion of Errol Tobias as the first non-white to start a game for the Springboks caused uproar in the troubled nation's divided communities for very different reasons.

Some activists felt that for a black man to represent a country while it was still practising apartheid was tantamount to condoning the system that discriminated against him. Others felt that he should never be allowed to play for South Africa because he was not white like the rest of the squad.

Tobias, who had already been playing rugby for ten years, admitted that his decision to wear the Springbok shirt was motivated by a sense of natural justice rather than any complex appraisal of the political implications. He explained later, 'I wanted to show the country and the rest of the world that black players could be just as good, if not better, than whites, and that if you are good enough you should play.'

He toured New Zealand with the Springboks and admitted to sensing 'tension' in other squad members at first; however, the barriers were slowly coming down and as fly-half Tobias played a pivotal role in his country's double thrashing of England in 1984. In six tests for the Springboks he scored 22 points. Significantly, he never finished on the losing side – not many white Springboks could say that. Errol had proved his point.

Errol Tobias

Born: 18 March 1950

Place of birth: Caledon, South Africa

Caps: 6

Teams: South Africa, South African Barbarians

LEGEND

Exciting but Painful

Zimbabwe Play in the First World Cup

1987 Given the rich history of rugby in the land now known as Zimbabwe, there was something fitting about its inclusion in the Inaugural Rugby World Cup. The oldest rugby clubs in Bulawayo, Queens and the Bulawayo Athletic Club, had been formed as far back as 1894, and the Rhodesian Rugby Football Union was formed a year later. British Isles touring teams had been there as early as 1910, when there was no reason to assume that the country would not become a major force in the world game.

Time and politics changed all that, but Zimbabwe were no less proud to be staking their claim to world recognition when the World Cup got under way in Australia and New Zealand. The setting for their first, and closest, contest could not have been more classic – Eden Park, Auckland, fortress of the All Blacks. Their opposition, Romania, looked less formidable and when Zimbabwe were 11-3 ahead by half-time a historic victory looked likely. Despite two piercing tries from centre Richard Tsimbo, it was not to be and Romania edged it 21-20, then Zimbabwe's World Cup went downhill. Scotland beat them 60-21, France won 70-12. World Cup 1987 had been an exciting but painful experience.

They reached World Cup 1991 in high spirits, until Ireland, Scotland and even Japan put more than 50 points on them. At least they were back on a big stage after all those years in the wilderness.

Opposite: Scotland's John Jeffrey races away from Zimbabwe in the match that was to be lost 60-21.

LANDMARK

On a Winning Streak

Namibia Beat Ireland and Italy – Twice

1991 Namibia will remember 1991 as the year they simply could not stop winning. Regrettably, given their stunning form, independence came too late to allow them to qualify for the Rugby World Cup, since they had only formed a rugby union and joined the International Board the previous year.

Up-and-coming Italy probably fancied their chances when they went down to Windhoek for a couple of matches in June 1991. They left deflated, having lost 17-7 and then 33-19.

Ireland might have treated those results as a warning but if they did, it hardly made much difference to their own fate a month later. Sam Stoop, the full back, scored Namibia's try in a historic 15-6 victory over a rugby nation respected the world over.

The African side's captain, Gerhard Mans, probably told his team to prepare for a backlash a week later when the teams met again. The backlash never came, largely because Namibia did not allow the Irish to dominate any area of the game. Instead, almost unbelievably, the new rugby nation ran in no fewer than 5 tries, with Mans and Stoop among the scorers.

Those were just some of the highlights of a year that saw Namibia win all ten of their tests, including five victories over rivals Zimbabwe and one against Portugal. Namibia have qualified for every World Cup since 1999, beating Morocco twice to reach the 2007 tournament.

Opposite: No backlash. Namibia's Eden Myer (left) and Johan Barnard (right) move in on Ireland's Brendan Mullin clutching a high ball in the second match against Ireland.

Abdel Benazzi

France's Moroccan Giant

1990s On 20 August 1968, one of the greatest rugby players the world has ever seen was born in Morocco. A giant from an early age, Abdel Benazzi started out as a soccer goalkeeper in his native Oujda. Then, as he filled out more, he threw the shot and discus for the local athletics club. By the time he turned sixteen, he was already pushing back scrum machines with the local men and he represented his African country before being adopted by France.

Benazzi played seventy-eight times for the French and led them to the 1997 Grand Slam, his second personal clean sweep. He was a World Cup finalist in 1999 and should have reached the same showpiece in 1995. In the last seconds of the semi-final against South Africa, he was adjudged to have fallen inches short of the try-line, when success would have knocked out the eventual winners. 'We were crying because we should have been there, but at least I made Nelson Mandela happy,' he said later.

With forty-eight test victories and nine tries, after his retirement in 2003, Benazzi could have been forgiven for sitting back to savour what he had achieved. Instead he decided to return to his African roots to set up the Noor Association, which encouraged Moroccan children to play sport – especially rugby. He felt Morocco had a great chance of qualifying for the 2007 World Cup in France, but his dream died in November 2006, when they lost to Namibia in a play-off.

Abdul Benazzi

Born: 20 August 1968

Place of birth: Oujda, Morocco

Caps: 78

Teams: Morocco, France, Saracens

LEGEND

Rhinos Fail to Find Their Feet

South Africa Thrashed by Fiji et al. (LEAGUE)

1995 They had been the Springboks, now they had been reinvented as the Rhinos, though they were still composed of former rugby union players. No matter, South Africa were handed a dream chance to play in the 1995 World Cup in England, and could not wait to test themselves against some of the best players on the planet.

The Rhinos were drawn to play in Group One, alongside Australia and England, but at least their first match was against a lesser-known rugby league nation, Fiji. With luck, the Rhinos could find their rhythm against Fiji and be at their very best to play the giants of the game.

It seemed a sensible plan and the Rhinos had every reason to feel confident as they burst out of the dressing room on to Cougar Park, Keighley. There was one problem – in the next eighty minutes, they were slaughtered 52-6 by the Fijians. It was a devastating blow to their hopes of winning respect for the sport back home; additionally, they had just two days to prepare for a match against the best team in the world, Australia.

Gateshead International Stadium near Newcastle, England was the scene of the humiliation. The final scoreline was Australia 86, South Africa 6. The only positive they could take from the match (apart from the fact that it was over) was that they had not been shut out entirely. Against England, that nightmare came true, with a 46-0 defeat. Played three, lost three; points for, twelve; points against, 184. South African rugby league has never fully recovered.

Opposite: England's Chris Joint evades South Africa's defence during the Rhinos' last crushing match in the 1995 Rugby League World Cup.

LANDMARK

Tragic Accident Highlights Danger

Max Brito of Ivory Coast Paralysed at World Cup

1995 The 1995 World Cup was a wonderful tournament but also a tragic one. Max Brito, the Ivory Coast winger, was running out of defence three minutes into his country's final group match against Tonga when he was tackled by their big-hitting forward, Inoke Afeaki. Brito was left vulnerable and twisted as more players piled on top of him. He did not move away from the melee with the others and everyone on the pitch knew that something very serious had happened as he continued to lie motionless for minutes. An air ambulance took Brito to Pretoria's Unitas hospital, where his life was saved, but no amount of intensive care could change the sad fact that his spinal injury would leave him paralysed and wheelchair-bound for the rest of his life.

In 1996, to raise money to give Brito a better life, Ghana hosted a match at the National Stadium in Accra, featuring teams from England and South Africa, including greats of the game, such as Dean Richards, Martin Johnson and Naas Botha. In 1999 Brito was guest of honour at the World Cup final in the Millennium Stadium, Cardiff.

Similar spinal injuries happen every year in rugby at different levels and the authorities are constantly looking at ways to minimize the danger. It is an inescapable fact that, by comparison to the ever-dangerous union game, rugby league's rules reduce the risk of spinal injuries significantly.

Opposite: Max Brito dives at Scotland's Craig Joiner,
eight days before the fateful match against Tonga.

LANDMARK

The Mandela Final

South Africa's Day

1995 The game itself was a low-scoring war of attrition but the build-up, climax and aftermath of the 1995 Rugby World Cup final were staggering in their dramatic power. South Africa's Joel Stransky dropped a late goal to beat New Zealand 15-12 and earn his country the world title in front of their own fans at Ellis Park. There was already a conspiracy theory attached to the victory. Later, New Zealand's coach, Laurie Mains, claimed that his team had been deliberately poisoned by a waitress serving coffee at a pre-match banquet.

Certainly the favourites were suffering from acute stomach problems before and during the match, and many All Blacks finished the game in a weakened state. The sight of New Zealand three-quarter Jeff Wilson rushing off to find a toilet in the middle of the match lingers in the memory. Yet it was never proven that a deliberately debilitating act had taken place.

One way or another, it was destined to be South Africa's day. When the final whistle blew, Francois Pienaar gathered his entire team in a circle, not to celebrate but to kneel and give thanks to God.

Nelson Mandela wore Pienaar's number six shirt when he presented the captain with the Webb Ellis Trophy, and thanked him for what he had done for South Africa. 'I have not done anything like as much as you, Mr President,' came his reply. 'Besides, we had forty-three million people helping us out there today.'

The Rainbow Nation, as Archbishop Desmond Tutu had called it, was born in some style.

'South Africa owes you a lot today.'

Nelson Mandela congratulating Francois Pienaar

LANDMARK

Francois Pienaar

Moving Rugby Union into a Professional Era

1995 Most famous for his leading role in the 1995 final, the rest of Francois Pienaar's remarkable story is often overlooked. It is easy to forget that when he took over South Africa's captaincy in 1993, he had never played for the Springboks before. He promptly skippered his country into troubled waters. There was defeat to France at home, another series reverse to Australia away, and little more than the consolation of back-to-back victories in Argentina to steady the ship. The following year, there was the frustration of a drawn series against England at home, then crushing defeats in New Zealand.

It is a testament to Pienaar's confidence, and his ability to maintain it in his players, that South Africa won in Scotland and Wales to go into the World Cup feeling they had a fighting chance. Even so, they were 9-1 outsiders, a pessimism that made the World Cup wins against Australia, Romania, Canada, Western Samoa, France and finally New Zealand all the more remarkable. Pienaar's easy chemistry with Nelson Mandela (who is godfather to one of his sons) made the sporting triumph all the more significant for the country he represented.

He made further rugby history when it was all over. By the time he retired in 1996, with twenty-nine caps, Pienaar had played a leading role in taking the entire game of rugby union into a new, professional era.

Francois Pienaar

Born: 2 January 1967
Place of birth: Vereeniging, South Africa
Caps: 29
Teams: South Africa, Transvaal Province, Saracens

LEGEND

Joel Stransky

Vital Last-Gasp Drop-Goal

1995 Like Jonny Wilkinson eight years later, Joel Stransky will for ever be remembered as the man who won the World Cup for his country with a last-gasp drop-goal. In fact, he kicked three of them during the 1995 tournament, but the effort that finally sank the mighty New Zealand is the only one that will go down in history. That decisive offering, to make it 15-12 to the new Rainbow Nation, was all the more admirable because Stransky had to think on his feet. A set move had just gone wrong, forcing him to improvise from an unplanned angle. He did so with aplomb.

The little maestro did not have huge experience of pressure on the biggest stage (his test debut against Australia coming only in 1993) but by the end of 1996, he had played his twenty-second and last test match, scoring a total of 6 tries and 240 points during his brief time in the sun.

An impressive switch to English club Leicester saw Stransky notch up 459 points in a single season, a Tigers record. There was even talk of the majestic fly-half turning out for England in the next World Cup, but he would not have qualified, and a knee injury forced him to retire that same year.

As he tried his luck at coaching, he knew he was one of the select few who could say it was their moment of excellence, when it really mattered, that won their country the Webb Ellis Trophy.

Joel Stransky

Born: 16 July 1967

Place of birth: Pietermaritzburg, South Africa

Caps: 23

Teams: South Africa, Leicester Tigers

LEGEND

Joost van der Westhuizen

More Glitter than Gareth Edwards

1900s–2000s

One of the few scrum-halves in rugby history who can lay claim to a more glittering career than the legendary Gareth Edwards, Joost van der Westhuizen has scored more test tries than any other number nine the game has known. He may not have possessed the spell-binding grace of Edwards in his prime, but 38 tries are proof of an unparalleled deadliness from behind the scrum. No South African player – not even a winger – has run in so many scores.

Tall for his position, strong, agile and fast, van der Westhuizen needed only a sniff of a chance to unleash one of his explosive trademark bursts to the try-line. There was something of the executioner in his cold blue eyes, and opposing sides grew to fear his exploitation of the slightest gap or weakness. Improvised blind-side raids with full-back André Joubert at his shoulder were particularly effective.

Unlike Stransky and Pienaar, van der Westhuizen went on to experience the 1999 World Cup and even the one after that before he retired in 2003. His ten-year reign had many highlights in attack; and yet his big hit on Jonah Lomu, who was considered unstoppable until the 1995 World Cup final, is most fondly remembered as a key moment in South Africa's finest hour.

Joost van der Westhuizen

Born: 20 February 1971

Place of birth: Pretoria, South Africa

Caps: 89

Teams: South Africa

LEGEND

Extinction Threat

Rhinos Lose to France (LEAGUE)

2000 & '01 The soap opera behind the South Africa Rhinos rugby league team did not get any happier at the start of the new millennium. First there was the Rugby World Cup in 2000, when they lost 40-8 to Wales and could still call it their best result. Then came a humiliating failure to score against Papua New Guinea, who had no such problems and won 16-0. Finally, in that same tournament, they were thrashed by Tonga, 66-18.

The very future of the Rhinos seemed to be on the line when they played two games against France in November 2001, seeking to restore their reputation. Sadly that did not happen. The French won the first match 44-6, and a week later reproduced the same sort of form to take a 48-8 victory. For the Rhinos, it seemed, there was nowhere left to go. Their lack of fixtures for future years was making it impossible to maintain credibility on a major world stage.

Four teams were still competing for the Tom Van Vollenhoven Cup in South Africa, and there was always the hope of a new, more successful, chapter in the international history of the country's rugby league team. For 2001, however, it looked as though the Rhinos were perilously close to extinction.

Opposite: Jerome Guisset of France is tackled by Hercules Erasmus and Jamie Blome (right) of South Africa during the Rugby League World Cup, November 2000, where the Rhinos lost 56-3.

LANDMARK

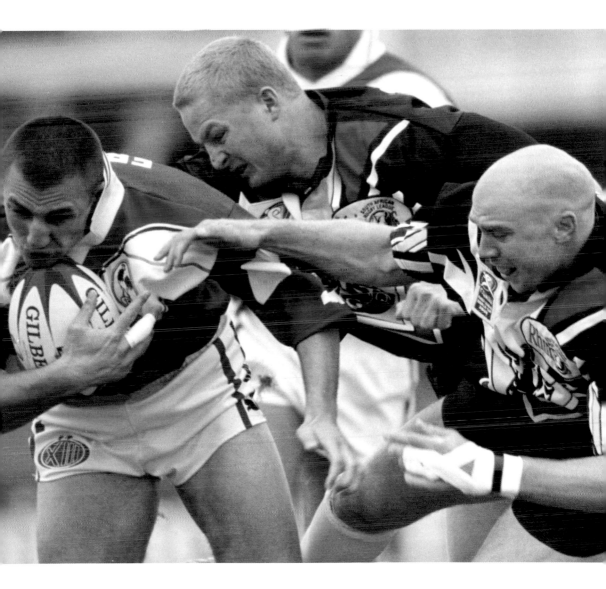

Percy Montgomery

Goal-Kicking Points Machine

2000s The most prolific points scorer in Springbok rugby history, Percy Montgomery understood the value of the boot from a painful conclusion to his very first test match in 1997, when the British Lions scored a narrow and dramatic victory in Durban. Montgomery made it his business to find the consistency and accuracy that would help him become a winner, and put him among rugby's finest ever goal-kicking technicians.

By 17 June 2006, when South Africa played a test against Scotland, Montgomery had become the first Springbok past 600 points, and soon he had more than twice the points total of his country's other great rugby marksman, Naas Botha. Montgomery, of course, had played far more matches, winning his eightieth cap that season, but it was still extraordinary success for a man who takes only one step before letting fly with his boot.

He was an integral part of the 1999 South Africa team that reached the World Cup semi-final in a brave attempt to defend their title. Australia put paid to that dream, but Montgomery, the Springboks' points machine from full-back, had his own place in history guaranteed.

Percy Montgomery

Born: 15 March 1974

Place of birth: Walvis Bay, South Africa

Caps: 80

Teams: South Africa, Natal Sharks, Newport RFC, Newport Gwent Dragons

LEGEND

AMERICAS

Many people were unaware that rugby was played in South America until 1972, when a plane carrying members of Uruguay's Old Christians Rugby Club to an exhibition match in Chile crashed into the Andes. Survivors were forced to eat human flesh until they were rescued from the mountains. The story, both horrific and inspiring, was turned into a best-selling book and a movie, *Alive*. After that, no one doubted that grass-roots rugby in South America had produced some very brave and resilient characters.

Mercifully there are other, less-troubling, reasons to remember rugby teams from the Americas and, happily, their achievements against all odds are expressed in a purely sporting context. From the USA's rugby gold medal at the 'Chariots of Fire' Olympics, to Canada's dramatic World Cup quarter-final against New Zealand, and more recently to Twickenham in 2006 (where Argentina beat England), Americas' rugby has created some powerful moments. Here are just a few.

Rugby Better Than Boston Game

First Recorded Rugby Match on American Soil

1874 It is thought that rugby was introduced to the USA by English soldiers and colonists some time in the mid-nineteenth century. By 1872 there were reports of several clubs thriving in the San Francisco Bay area, without any competition actually taking place. The first recorded rugby match on American soil resulted from a hastily-accepted challenge by a Harvard captain called Harry Grant, who agreed to play the game with McGill University of Montreal, if their students would first play Harvard at the 'Boston' game, a cross between soccer and what later turned into American Football.

All was going so well for Harvard when the teams played to their own rules that the Americans decided to spare their Canadian guests any more punishment at 3-0. With their pride dented, McGill's young men trudged off warning, 'Wait until tomorrow when we play rugby.' The Harvard team maintained their composure until left alone, at which point one asked 'What's rugby?' Much later, another team member recalled how frantically they prepared for battle the next day, ' ...we went to work to learn the Rugby game, but I should question if there were three men in the college who had ever seen the egg-shaped ball. A drop-kick was an unknown, an incredible feat, and the intricacies of off-side and free-kick seemed inextricable mysteries to novices like us.'

They caught on quickly and managed to prevent scoring on 15 May 1874, the historic day that first game was played. The Harvard team were so proud of their rugby 0-0 that they forgot all about the 'Boston' game and the following autumn headed off to Montreal in search of more rugby. By then 'touchdowns' were allowed and Harvard scored 3 to register an American team's first rugby victory.

Opposite: Harvard University's historic college yard in Cambridge, Massachusetts.

LANDMARK

Argentina's Debut in World Rugby

Argentina 3 Combined Britain 28

1910 It says much for the spirit of adventure, not to mention the strength in depth of British rugby at this early stage that, while one British Isles team was touring South Africa in 1910, another was taking Argentina by storm. Organized through contacts at Oxford University, with a backbone of Englishmen and a few Scots thrown in, the Great Britain XV (or Combined Britain, as they were also known) meant business from the start.

They played six matches in Argentina in a mere three weeks from late May to mid-June. Captained by John E. Raphael, who would later be killed at Remy during World War I, the British started with a 19-13 win over Argentina A, which proved to be their toughest examination.

The tour itinerary was planned carefully, because Argentina might have caught them cold if the South Americans had been allowed to throw their strongest side at Great Britain while their guests were still finding their feet. As it was, Belgrano, Argentina B and Buenos Aires were all soundly beaten before it came to the big match on 12 June. The intriguingly initialled F. de C.M. Heriot (there seems to be no record of his full name) had the satisfaction of grounding Argentina's first try in the international arena. Oswald Gebbie led the home side bravely as they fought to stay in the game but the British were too strong, and ran in a total of 5 tries. H.G. Monks scored 2, while W.L. Fraser, H.E. Ward and Great Britain's captain, Raphael, completed the rout.

There could be no complaints, and Argentina Natives were the last to fall to the tourists, 41-10. The Combined 'Invincibles' had fulfilled their mission, and it would be a long time before Argentina learned to compete with the giants of world rugby.

Opposite: Hertford College, Oxford University. The team put together by this university gave Argentina their first chance at international rugby.

LANDMARK

USA Win Olympic Rugby Gold

With Ugly Scenes in Europe

1920 & '24 If they made a Hollywood blockbuster about the USA rugby team of the early twenties, people would not believe it. The Americans really did win rugby gold twice at the Olympics, a double for which they were nearly lynched.

Although rugby union had not been played competitively in America for more than a decade, it would be wrong to suggest that the USA team, put together by the Universities of Stanford and Santa Clara, were a bunch of sporting innocents. Daniel Carroll had won gold with Australia in previous games, Morris Kirksey was so fast that he also won silver in the 100 yards dash, and gold again in the 4 x 100 yards relay. Robert Templeton, also of Stanford, would go on to become a famous track coach. For 1920, all they had to do was remember how to play rugby. Their golden victory of 8-0 against the French favourites suggests they had retained some grasp of the rules.

Still feeling sore in 1924, the French demanded that the dormant Americans (who were by then without a game for years), defend their title in Paris. Seven of the old team recruited a few younger men and set sail for Europe. Both the USA and France dished out sound beatings to Romania, though the hosts were 20-1 odds-on favourites for the gold medal. The atmosphere was ugly and the Americans were spat at and abused every time they left their hotel in the build-up to the final.

Fifty thousand fanatical supporters went to see their side triumph but when they had to watch the USA running in 5 tries instead, they began to beat American fans senseless and throw them towards waiting ambulances near the touchline. One America player, Norman Cleaveland, recalled, 'I thought we were dead. They were throwing bottles and rocks and clawing at us through the fence.' As a shock 17-3 win was secured, an American replacement called Gideon Nelson was flattened by a walking stick. His team-mate, Charles Doe, remembered, 'The medal ceremony took place in front of tens of thousands of people who wanted to rip us to shreds.'

Opposite: the American rugby team of the 1920 Antwerp Olympics.

LANDMARK

The Pumas are Born

Argentina's First Overseas Tour

1965 When the animal on your team crest is mistaken for another beast entirely, it must be tempting to correct the offender before the wrong idea is passed on once more. On their first foreign tour in 1965, Argentina won maximum marks for diplomacy, when they adopted the name of the animal that had been quite wrongly associated with them. Argentina were in South Africa, proudly wearing their UAR (Unión Argentina de Rugby) blazers complete with jaguar motif. A journalist who clearly did not know one big cat from another, and desperate for a catchy name to go with the Springboks, Wallabies and Lions, called Argentina the Pumas. Rather than cause trouble, the tourists simply went with the new name, while retaining the jaguar on their blazers. Thus Argentina's nickname was born, along with their dangerous reputation.

South Africa had not paid their guests the ultimate respect of fielding their strongest side in the big match and they were to regret that overconfidence. It was the Junior Springboks, captained by a twenty-seven-year-old lock called Aitor Otona, who ran out on to Ellis Park in Johannesburg to show the South Americans what rugby was all about.

By the end of the match, Argentina were dishing out the lessons. Tries by their dynamic flanker, Raul Loyola, Eduardo Espana on the wing, and a utility back named Marcelo Pascual gunned down the Springboks in front of their own startled supporters. Eduardo Poggi converted one of the scores, and Argentina's Pumas had written their first happy chapter in rugby history.

Opposite: Argentina playing their very first match away from South America, against Rhodesia, on 8 May 1965. Though they lost 17-12, Argentina showed flashes of the class that would shine through against South Africa.

LANDMARK

Rugby's Biggest Tragedy

Old Christians of Uruguay Forced to Eat Human Flesh

1972 The Old Christians Rugby Club of Carrasco had earned their reputation as one of the finest teams in their part of South America. These old-boys from the Stella Maris School of Montevideo won the National Championship in Uruguay in 1968 and 1970, then spread their wings to find new challenges. A successful tour to Chile in 1971 was to be followed by another the following year. Players persuaded friends and relations to join them for extra numbers to keep the cost of expensive individual flight tickets down to an acceptable level. Forty-five people, including crew, boarded a plane on Friday, 13th October for what was to be its final journey over the Andes. The second tour to Chile never happened.

Thirteen were killed instantly when Uruguayan Air Force Flight 571 crashed, and three more died of their wounds that night in the freezing mountains. Nine days later, with those still alive starving to death, most decided to try to survive by eating some of the flesh from the dead bodies. For eight people, the trauma in making that decision was, ultimately, futile when their lives were lost in an avalanche on the night of the 29th. Most of the rest resorted to the desperate measures for their chance of life. As the weeks went by, and it became clear that no help was coming, some of the more seriously injured gently slipped away. By mid-December there were only sixteen left alive with no apparent way out. Eventually, after at least one failed attempt, Fernando Parrado and Roberto Canessa climbed the surrounding peaks and spotted a possible path down towards green vegetation, the sort that might support animals and a few human beings far below. With their last remaining energy, they followed their instincts and brought rescue to their friends. It was 22 December and the main group were enduring their third month of hell when the first helicopters arrived. From that day it has been almost impossible to think of Uruguayan rugby without remembering the bravery of the Old Christians.

'They were ordinary young men driven to the very limits of human endurance.'

Tagline of the film about the tragedy, Alive

LANDMARK

Premature Celebrations

South American Jaguars Beat the Springboks

1982 It is never a good idea to celebrate victory too hard before the job is fully done. Most rugby players learn this rule during their schooldays, usually to their great embarrassment. In 1982 it was a Springbok team in South Africa, the country that has perhaps taken the game more seriously than any other, that was guilty of such a basic mistake. They were playing the South American Jaguars, who, controversially in the eyes of many, were alleviating the isolation imposed on South Africa by the sporting community due to apartheid. To avoid a backlash, the Jaguars were not playing under a fixed national banner but, led by Hugo Porta (already thirty-one), they were almost all Argentinian.

When the team first formed to play South Africa in 1980, there were players from Uruguay, Paraguay, Chile, Peru and even Brazil. Five defeats had followed, both in South Africa and South America, and the make-up of the side in 1982 was not quite so diverse as before. Not that the Argentinian backbone of the team was bringing much success on this particular tour. In the first test in Pretoria, the Springboks destroyed the South Americans 50-18. There was one match to go – a return test in Bloemfontein a week later. The South Africans did not see how the tourists could hurt them; they partied and relaxed, feeling the job was done.

Porta was not ready to concede defeat – he had brought his team a long way under difficult political circumstances and he wanted to leave the Springboks something to remember him by. In Bloemfontein, he left a try, which he converted, a drop-goal and 4 penalties as parting gifts. The South Africans were in no shape to return the compliment. Porta had scored all 21 points in a shock 21-12 victory. The Springboks would never again be so keen to celebrate prematurely.

Opposite: Hugo Porta, star scorer of the Bloemfontein match, lays on a pass for one of his team-mates during a game against the England XV in 1978, which ended 13-13.

LANDMARK

A Draw That Demanded Respect

Argentina 21 All Blacks 21

1985 There have been many wonderfully shocking moments during Argentina's time in world rugby: the 24-13 victory over Australia in 1979 or the 19-19 draw with England in 1981, when Clive Woodward scored 2 tries to give his side a share of the spoils. The Pumas beat Australia again, this time 18-3 in Brisbane, and took the scalp of France in 1985, by 24-16. However, the surprise everybody seems to remember most fondly is Argentina's dramatic draw with the All Blacks in Buenos Aires.

Perhaps it was because the All Blacks were such a great side, and two years later they were to make the entire world acknowledge that greatness at the Inaugural Rugby World Cup; or because New Zealand led 18-9 at half-time against the Pumas (and very few return to have a meaningful say against them once they have taken command to that extent). Most of all, however, people remember what happened with such affection because an unfancied side, which depended on a thirty-four-year-old veteran for a glimmer of hope, refused to bow to the seemingly inevitable, and launched a scarcely believable comeback.

The desperate ferocity of the Pumas' pack, as it sought to hold its own against the mighty All Blacks' forwards, contrasted perfectly with the classy nonchalance of Porta at fly-half, as his casual boot undid all New Zealand's work. Slowly, but surely, it was Porta who took control away from the strongest side in the business; and it was Porta who showed how, given any kind of platform, he possessed a weapon that was all but unplayable – his drop-goal. Three times Porta put New Zealand to the sword this way, and 4 penalties from the same source gave Argentina the draw they so richly deserved. It did not mean the Pumas had earned a share of the series, but that did not seem to matter. That extraordinary draw in 1985 earned Argentina as much respect worldwide as all the previous wins put together.

Opposite: Hugo Porta continues to put up a fight against the All Blacks in 1987.

LANDMARK

Hugo Porta

Drop-Goal King

1970s–80s

No one has ever made drop-goals look quite so easy, so often, as Argentina's Hugo Porta. In fifty-five matches for the Pumas, he calmly slotted 25 drop-goals to sap the spirits of even the toughest sides. There were three in the victory over Australia in 1979, when Porta scored 16 of his side's 24 points; another three against the mighty All Blacks. No team was safe from Porta's secret weapon; and even when it was no longer a secret, there was very little any opponent could do to stop it.

Given that Argentina have never been among the world's top-ranked sides, it is a tribute to Porta's grace and balance under pressure that he amassed 529 points, including 88 penalties and 78 conversions. His 10 tries do not match the tally of many in his position, but Porta was more than capable of releasing his three-quarters when the moment was right. His relaxed style and economy of effort meant that Porta was able to continue to make a huge impact in the international arena long after others would have hung up their boots. When he captained Argentina to the first World Cup in 1987, he was thirty-six years old. Still he managed to inspire his country to their first World Cup win, by 25-16 against Italy. Porta came out of retirement when he was nearly forty for internationals against Ireland, England and Scotland in 1990 and he did not look out of place.

However, a political career beckoned and he was made Argentina's ambassador to South Africa the following year. By 1994 he was Minister for Sport. He had come a long way since making his debut for the Pumas in 1971; that priceless kicking boot had always taken him wherever he wanted to go.

Hugo Porta

Born: 11 September 1951
Place of birth: Buenos Aires, Argentina
Caps: 65
Teams: Banco Nación, Argentina, South American Jaguars

LEGEND

American World Cup Glory

USA Eagles Beat Japan 21-18 in First World Cup

1987 From the 1874 rugby craze at Harvard, through to the Olympic triumphs of 1920 and 1924, it seemed as though Americans needed only to take the game seriously for a while to beat all challengers. If only the US Eagles found life that simple towards the end of the twentieth century.

There were encouraging moments, such as the hard-earned 3-3 draw with Canada in Albany, 1982, or the 9-9 draw with Japan in Torrance, 1986; but there were also tougher times, such as a 49-3 thrashing in Sydney, 1983. Still, the Americans must have been doing something right, because they received an invitation to take part in the inaugural World Cup in Australia and New Zealand in 1987. When they discovered they were in the same group as Australia and England, they must have known, deep down, that those games would be an exercise in damage limitation.

There was another team in that group – Japan – and for the Eagles it would make their World Cup final. Evenly matched, both teams knew that victory might depend on who wanted it most and who could come up with a nerveless match-winner on the day. When 24 May 1987 dawned Down Under, the man who rose to the occasion was the Eagles' full-back, Ray Nelson. Glasgow-born and twenty-five-years old, Nelson was at the peak of his powers that day, half way through a career that would see him win twenty-five caps between 1983 and 1991. He supplied that special something that was needed to sink the proud Japanese. Nelson scored a try, converted it along with those from Gary Lambert and Mike Purcell, and kicked a penalty that would prove the difference between the teams.

The Eagles' captain, Ed Burlington, was nearly thirty-five and try-scorer Purcell had already passed that birthday. Nelson had given them a moment of glory before it was too late and his country a World Cup victory to go with those other great snapshots from history.

Opposite: American Joe Clarkson, second right, dives as he passes the ball during the first half of the game in which the USA beat Japan.

LANDMARK

A Moment Too Soon

Canada Beat USA at Rugby League

1987 Sport can be tough when you never beat your closest rivals but at least the incentive endures when a struggling team seeks the magic ingredient that will bring about the elusive win. The problem for the Canada Cougars, as the country's rugby league team later became known, was that their greatest moment came too soon and they spent their remaining existence desperately trying to remember what they had done right.

At the start of 1987, Canada had never played a rugby league international but they put together a side to play the USA in Pittsburgh, Pennsylvania. The remarkable outcome was a 23-10 victory for the Canadians and those back home who cared rejoiced whole-heartedly. The feel-good factor contributed to the early success of a four-team league that saw Kingston (Ontario), Montreal (Ontario), Montreal (Quebec) and Adirondacks (New York State USA) start to pit their wits against each other on a regular basis.

Meanwhile, on the international front there was mounting frustration for the Canadians, as a second win against the Americans simply would not come. Instead they suffered nine heavy defeats against their rivals in a row, culminating in their 68-0 annihilation in the year 2000.

Although a Rugby Canada Super League was set up in 1998, the world is still waiting for Canada to do something super again, just like they did in 1987. The poor national team seemed to run out of opponents back in 2001 – but you never can say never in rugby.

Opposite: A Canadian supporter full of spirit.

LANDMARK

Worldwide Respect Won

Canada Reach World Cup Quarter-Finals

1991 Feisty to the point of outright aggression, full of forward passion and three-quarter panache, Canada were the most refreshing force at World Cup 1991, where they surprised everyone by storming into the quarter-finals.

A try from the Canucks' Vancouver-born full-back, Scott Stewart, and 3 penalties from the reassuring boot of Gareth Rees at the Stade Jean Douger in Bayonne was enough to outclass Fiji 13-3 in their opener.

The showdown with Romania in Toulouse provided the ideal platform for Canada's Glaswegian flanker, 'Gord' MacKinnon, who scored a fine try and fast became one of the tournament's outstanding players. It was a huge task against France in their own back yard, but Mark Wyatt went over for a try and also kicked a penalty in Agen, to go with a drop-goal and another penalty from Rees.

It may not have been enough for victory, but the 13-19 reverse was more than respectable and their excellent group performances set up a dream quarter-final against the rugby giants of New Zealand. Not for a second in that rain-swept quarter-final at Lille did the Canadians give an inch, and their pugnacious display almost boiled over into something more controversial as tempers flared.

A young Al Charron, who led Canada into World Cup 2003 twelve years later, had reason to be proud of his try, as did the scrum-half, Chris Tynan. In the end, the powerful know-how of the New Zealanders won through. A 29-13 defeat marked the end of a glorious adventure, but Canada had won new respect worldwide.

Opposite: The 1991 Rugby World Cup captains before a World Cup welcome dinner at the Royal Lancaster Hotel, London. Canada's Mark Wyatt stands out in his red blazer.

LANDMARK

Gareth Rees

Sixth in Rugby's Ranks of Great Point-Scorers

1990s Canada's greatest player, Gareth Rees became the first man from any country to star in four World Cups between 1987 and 1999. He was only twenty-four at the 1991 tournament and yet he gave the fiery Canadians immense authority with his clever kicking. Asked if reaching the World Cup quarter-final that year was the highlight of his career, he once said, 'No, it was getting my first cap in 1986 at High Cobbet Field in Tuscon, Arizona, one of the great rugby pitches of the world.'

There would be fifty-five caps in all and 487 points, although some record books put his tally even higher at 493. Whoever is right, that amazing total puts Rees sixth in the all-time rankings of the game's great point-scorers. Rees put in some massive individual displays for Canada over the years, not least when he scored 16 points as Wales were humbled in their own National Stadium in Cardiff.

There were moments of controversy too, and Rees was sent off for fighting with players from the host nation, South Africa, at the World Cup in 1995. The incident did not seem to affect his long-term composure when the posts were in range and he was top-scorer during England's club seasons of 1996 and 1997.

His career took him from Castaways in Canada to Oxford University, Wasps and Harlequins in England, over Merignac in France and also to Newport in Wales. Whether at fly-half or full-back, he managed to influence matches even when he began to put on weight towards the end of his career. Rees, the rugby natural, was missed by Canada when he finally retired.

Gareth Rees

Born: 30 June 1967

Place of birth: Duncan, British Columbia

Caps: 55

Teams: Castaways, Wasps, Harlequins, Merignac, Newport, Oxford University, Bedford, Barbarians, Canada

LEGEND

Federico Mendez

Passionate About the Pumas

1990s One of the finest front-row stars the modern game ever knew, Federico Mendez exploded on to the international scene with a peach of a punch at Twickenham in 1990. He was eighteen and playing for Argentina against England, when he connected so sweetly with Paul Ackford's jaw that the England lock was knocked clean out. Unfortunately for Mendez, this was rugby not boxing and he was sent straight off. Ackford staggered to his feet but his legs had turned to jelly. He was nicknamed 'Bambi' and 'Glassjaw' for the rest of his career, a dubious reward for taking a blow that even Mendez admitted he did not deserve. The young Argentinian claimed he had been gunning for Jeff Probyn, and alleged that the Wasps prop had provoked him. Mendez was too good a player, whether playing as a hooker or a prop, to allow a reputation for thuggery to define him for long. He terrified even the most hardened of opposing front rows with his awesome power and technique. And 13 tries in his first sixty-seven internationals showed that he was deadly in the loose as well as at set-pieces.

'Freddie' doesn't always choose his words carefully, and after playing under the future England coach Andy Robinson at Bath he concluded, 'Andy wasn't the nicest guy but then I wasn't always in a good mood either.' By the time he reached thirty-three, Mendez had chalked up eighty-three caps for his country, and his leathery face looked more fearsome with every passing year. The Springboks paid Freddie the ultimate compliment of offering him a post as their scrum coach, but Mendez declined, explaining that he could not bear the thought of helping any country overcome his beloved Argentina. That was Mendez.

Federico Mendez

Born: 2 August 1972

Place of birth: Argentina

Caps: 74

Teams: Bath Rugby, Northampton Saints

LEGEND

Proud Moment for Canada

Canada Beat Wales 26-24 at Cardiff

1993 One of the proudest moments in Canadian rugby history came with just seconds left on the clock in Cardiff in 1993, and Wales still 24-19 ahead. Al Charron, the rampaging forward who would go on to become Canada's most capped player, crashed over as if his life depended on it, and Gareth Rees was left with a nerve-testing conversion for glory. The fact that he was about to join a Welsh club, Newport, might have entered the mind of a less-experienced campaigner, but Rees remained cold and indifferent to his surroundings as he focused on the swing of his boot, and calmly kicked Canada to a historic victory. It was no more than the tourists deserved, because the try-count was two to zero.

Neil Jenkins had kicked all Wales's points, while the Canucks' captain, Ian Stuart, had already gone over for his country's first. For the Welsh, it was a disappointing debut from their giant forward, Scott Quinnell and there was a post-match inquest into a breakdown in communication between their coach, Alan Davies, and the fly-half, Adrian Davies. It is doubtful whether any change of tactics could have overshadowed the Canadians' superior desire. Nothing boosts a team's morale better than knowing that pressure is going to be turned into points almost every time. With 4 penalties and 2 conversions, Rees was supreme; however, even he must have felt the tension before taking that last, decisive kick.

Opposite: Al Charron, Canada's most capped player
and rampaging forward.

LANDMARK

Argentina's Biggest Win

Argentina 152 Paraguay 0

2002 There has never been a more one-sided match than this game played at Mendoza Rugby Club in the South American Championship on 1 May 2002. For Paraguay it might as well have been 1 April because it must have felt as though the rugby gods were playing a cruel joke when the true extent of the massacre became clear.

Try upon try, 24 in all, broke their resistance completely but still Argentina did not let up. Facundo Soler from Cordoba was the most ruthless, running in 5 tries from his prime position on the wing. Jose Nuñez Piossek made almost as much use of the space on the other flank to dive over 4 times. There were hat-tricks for Hernan Senillosa, Pedro Sporleder and Bernardo Stortoni, though scoring a mere 3 tries did not guarantee a player headlines on this particular day of destruction.

Ten players touched down in all, so it was easier to focus on the Argentinian players who did not get one. The fly-half, José Cilley, was such a player, and he was either extremely unselfish or too tired out to run very far after having to attempt so many conversions. Sixteen were landed successfully. Argentina have always been the strongest rugby nation in South America, but this was a day when the gap in class between top dog and some of the wannabes really went beyond a joke.

Opposite: Argentina's passion is evident in Jose Nuñez Piossek.

LANDMARK

World Cup Heartbreak

Argentina 15 Ireland 16

2003 It has often been thought that Argentina possessed the talent to take the World Cup by storm and 2003 was no exception. By the time the Pumas played Ireland at the Adelaide Oval, both sides needed to win in order to progress in the competition. From the first-half action, it seemed that the South Americans would have the edge. Gonzalo Quesada gave them the lead and went on to kick 3 penalties and a rather messy – but no less accurate – drop-goal. Argentina played the brighter rugby before the interval, yet it was Alan Quinlan of Ireland who stormed over for what proved to be the only try of the game, dislocating his shoulder in the process.

The Pumas knew they had what it takes to make an impact that year and a towering drop-goal from Ignacio Corleto, the Buenos Aires-born full-back, gave them renewed hope. Ronan O'Gara landed 2 penalties to restore Ireland's command of a still-unstable situation. Quesada hit back with his own boot and Agustin Pichot's Argentina fought their way to within one point of their opponents. The final whistle ended their late charge and broke the hearts of Puma supporters.

One year Argentina will probably do something truly extraordinary at the World Cup, but in 2003 it was not to be, and they could barely contain their disappointment.

Opposite: Ireland's John Hayes consoles Argentina's distraught Roberto Grau.

A Tale to Tell the Grandchildren

USA Almost Beats Australia at Rugby League

2004 The mere thought is staggering, yet in 2004 the impossible very nearly happened. At one stage in the match between the USA Tomahawks and the Australia Kangaroos at Franklin Field, the greatest upset in rugby league history looked inescapable. The Tomahawks were 18-0 ahead and still leading 24-6 at half-time – if they could just hold on, the mostly amateur American team would have something to tell their grandchildren, and anyone else who would listen, for the rest of their days.

How the World Cup and Tri-Nations champions, fielding a very strong side, got into that mess became clear afterwards. Their coach Wayne Bennett explained, 'We thought it would be a "turn up and we'll be OK" but that wasn't the case.' Rather arrogantly, unless you admire his honesty, Australia's second-rower, Ben Kennedy, said, 'It was pretty tough mentally. It's hard to get going in these matches when you know you're going to win.'

By the time Tomahawks tearaways Matt Petersen, Nate Smith, Ben Kelly and Brandon Costin had run the Roos ragged with first-half tries, the tourists were no longer certain of winning at all. They were embarrassed and talked at the break about how this was looking on television back home.

Mark O'Meley of the Bulldogs had torn knee ligaments, Darren Lockyer was taking big hits, and the kings of rugby league were in disarray as five thousand fans looked on in disbelief. Matt Bowen, scorer of Australia's only first-half offering, went on to hit the Americans with a hat-trick, while Shaun Berrigan, Matt Cooper and Willie Mason made certain of a 36-24 victory. Mason, a legendary hard man, had to limp off with a sore toe.

This was no ordinary day in rugby league. The Tomahawks' heroes will still dine out on the story for the rest of their lives – a tale of how they *nearly* beat the world's finest side.

'We almost shocked the world'

Jeff Preston, USA Tomahawks captain

LANDMARK

Lions' First Home-Turf Warm-up

Argentina 25 British and Irish Lions 25

2005 This match was historic because the Lions had never played a warm-up match in their own country before and had never sung the 'Power of Four' as an anthem. Neither had they ever looked quite so disorganized as they did when faced with this classy Argentina team.

The Pumas will remember being the first to tame the Lions that year, before a tour to New Zealand proved unsuccessful for the British and Irish party. More than anything, however, the Argentinians will recall how they should have made the occasion even more historic, from their point of view, by winning the match. So dominant were the Pumas at set-pieces that they forced 5 turnovers, as the Lions' scrum was smashed and their line-out jumpers dwarfed. Jose Nuñez Piossek took just four minutes to score Argentina's try, darting down the right to touch down almost before the home team knew what was happening. The inspired boot of Federico Todeschini helped the Pumas to take a 13-0 lead before Jonny Wilkinson's goal-kicking prowess began to work its own kind of magic.

Ollie Smith's try for the Lions was a rare high-point as Argentina looked capable of pulling off an upset right to the last. With a conversion and no fewer than 6 penalties, Todeschini was scoring points for fun, but his 20-point haul was not quite enough for victory. Typically, Wilkinson had the last say to match Todeschini's tally, though the moral victory definitely belonged to the plucky Pumas. Argentina would make Britain an even happier hunting ground before very long.

Opposite: Argentina's Nicolas Fernandez (right) crashes in a tackle on the Lions' Lewis Moody during the match that in their eyes they should have won.

LANDMARK

Heavy Defeat, Bitter Recriminations

Argentina Play and Lose First Rugby League Match

2005 Argentina's first tentative effort to introduce itself to the world of international rugby league ended in heavy defeat and bitter recriminations in March 2005. Their fledgling national team played two matches against Australia Police Rugby League, a highly respected outfit who expected to be given the sort of facilities they were used to back home before playing the 'Tests' in South America.

Unfortunately, the Aussie Police tour report later that year expressed 'bitter disappointment' with Argentina's efforts as hosts, and explained, 'The training grounds and playing fields were nowhere near what they were supposed to be and the hosts did not deliver. The training ground facilities were non-existent.' However, it did not seem to affect the outcome of the matches adversely, because the Australians won the first showdown 40-4, and the second by an even more convincing 50-6.

Staying in Buenos Aires seemed to agree with the trail-blazing tourists on some level at least; even so, the Australian Police passed their grievances on to the International Rugby League President, Colin Love, while carefully pointing out that they had still managed to enjoy themselves despite the drawbacks. 'We always have a good time, the nightlife and locals were very good to us,' said the tour report. 'We were the first ever to tour Argentina and represent Australia there.'

Unfortunately they risked being the last. With no figurehead to form an official rugby league organization, and no one to take the game forward, it appears that a brave Argentinian experiment may not have resulted in lasting success.

Opposite: Vibrant Buenos Aires. Though its rugby pitches were not up the scratch, its bars and people offered the Australians some enjoyment.

LANDMARK

Positive Outlook for Pumas

Argentina Clinch First Ever Win at Twickenham

2006 There have been more than a few 'nearlies' in the history of South American rugby but on 11 November 2006 Argentina achieved something fresh and definitive that can never be taken away from them. With a storming performance from their captain, Agustin Pichot, and a majestic contribution from Federico Todeschini, the Pumas registered their first win at Twickenham against the world champions. No one could say it was not deserved.

Paul Sackey's try put England 10-9 ahead at half-time; however, Argentina were already bubbling and it was only a matter of time before they came to the boil. Todeschini provided the red-hot running, a seventy-metre dash to the try-line after intercepting Toby Flood's careless pass. With a conversion of his try and 5 penalties, the Montpelier magician scored 22 points in Argentina's stunning 25-18 win.

Felipe Conteponi had earlier slotted a simple penalty in front of the posts to send England advance warning of what was to come. This was supposed to be the match in which England halted a terrible slide that had already seen six consecutive defeats. Iain Balshaw tried to launch a comeback with his own impressive try, but Argentina made sure their hosts suffered loss number seven to equal England's all-time record for rugby misery.

The Pumas had taken big scalps before, but this victory was a new landmark, an indication that they were still growing in strength as a rugby nation and more than capable of knocking some of the big boys on the world stage back down to size. It was a fitting way to end the year and an exciting time to be looking ahead. The world order in international rugby, as with the rest of life, can never be taken for granted. That, of course, is what makes world rugby such a winner.

'We knew if we put England under pressure in the second half they could crack.'

Argentina captain Agustin Pichot

LANDMARK

ASIA

Ask a rugby fan to think of Asia and one venue leaps to mind – Hong Kong. The reason, of course, is that mother of all rugby parties, the Hong Kong Sevens. This is the tournament where a true genius can break clear with a cheeky dummy or glorious side-step, then stretch his legs and simply show off the speed with which he has been blessed. Free from any serious responsibilities to country or team should a risky move backfire, the most entertaining players, from David Campese to Christian Cullen, have unleashed their dreams on an equally daring opposition. The spectacular setting, combined with the raucous sounds of frenzied fans from all over the world having the times of their lives, leaves a lasting impression. No one lucky enough to experience the show ever forgets it.

Yet Asia never ceases to surprise or mesmerize. In 2006, for example, Campese's international try-scoring record was beaten by a magician from Japan, Daisuke Ohata. As we shall see, this relatively untapped continent has already found many ways to make its mark on the rugby world.

Rugby First Introduced to Japan

Cambridge Graduates Teach Keio Students

1899 The origins of rugby in Japan owe much to the Universities of Oxford and Cambridge, and first past the post on this occasion was Cambridge. Edward Bramwell Clarke was born in Yokohama in 1875, the son of a baker, and towards the end of the nineteenth century he studied at Cambridge University, along with Tanaka Ginnosuke. By 1899, Clarke was back in Japan, teaching English at Keio University. To the returning intellectual, it seemed that his students had too much time on their hands and were wasting the golden autumn weather that had been so ideal for rugby back in England. Why not inject some vigour into his students' lives by teaching them rugby?

He enlisted the help of his fellow graduate, Ginnosuke, and soon began the first organized teaching of rugby in Japan. There is evidence to suggest that rugby matches had been played in Japan as far back as 1874, the year before Clarke was born, in treaty ports such as Kobe and Yokohama. Those were spontaneous affairs, thrown together with the help of visiting sailors' crews, not a measured attempt to introduce a piece of British sporting culture to a Japanese educational environment.

It cannot be said that rugby caught on early in twentieth century Japan, though Clarke coached it at Keio until a leg injury forced him to stop in 1910, but his contribution was a sound start. Cambridge University's timeless rivals were soon to provide fresh impetus.

Opposite: King's College, Cambridge. Cambridge University educated some of the first individuals who would introduce their coveted game of rugby to Japan.

Chichibu's Passion for Rugby

Japan Rugby Football Union (JRFU) Formed

1926 Prince Chichibu, the brother of Emperor Hirohito, was a young man who went on to develop dangerous militarist ambitions. Before he did so, Chichibu had an extraordinary passion for rugby, growing from his student days at Magdalen College, Oxford in 1925. It is not known how aware he was of the sport during his adolescence in Japan but when he first witnessed a British match, played in all its brutal beauty, he knew that he wanted his own countrymen to learn to play the same way.

Although Chichibu did not pursue a playing career at Oxford, he made it his business to learn the intricacies of the game and its administration. By the following year, 1926, he made it clear that the formation of a Japan Rugby Football Union, to be run along the lines of its English counterpart, would have his firm support. By 30 November 1926, the Prince's will had been done.

Rugby was popular only among the elite and struggled to capture the imagination of a wider sporting generation, so Japan's was not the busiest of RFUs in the following decades. However, a draw with British Columbia in 1930 and two impressive victories over Canada in 1932 set the ball rolling. Today, the JRFU offices are still located in the Chichibunomiya Stadium in Tokyo, named after the rugby-loving prince, and it remains very much Japanese rugby's spiritual home.

Opposite: Prince and Princess Chichibu with their entourage.

A Warning to the Rugby World

Japan 3 England 6

1971 In the English RFU's Centenary year, the English nearly suffered the embarrassment of losing to Japan in Tokyo, thanks to the Asian side's shrewd coach, Onishi Tetsunosuke. Sometimes described as 'a Japanese Carwyn James,' Tetsunosuke watched carefully when the England XV, who did not win caps on the tour, beat his side 19-27 in the first match. Japan had bagged 2 tries in that game, including 1 from their number eight, Yoshiro Murata, while Ryoji Yamaguchi had kicked 11 points before the home team were overwhelmed. If he could just tighten his defence, Tetsunosuke reasoned, Japan would have a chance to pull off one of rugby's biggest shocks in the next match, in four days' time.

He instilled his ideas in his players and by the time Japan's captain, Itoh Tadayuki, led his team out on to the pitch at the Chichibunomiya Stadium, the forwards believed that they could give the English more of a battle up front. So it proved, and the match was in the balance all the way to the final whistle. In the end, however, Ryoji Yamaguchi's solitary penalty was not quite enough to carry the day, though the moral victory certainly belonged to the improving Japanese.

The closeness of the result was noticed around the rugby world, and the major rugby-playing nations knew they could not afford to take victory for granted in this particular outpost any more. Some countries took more notice than others.

Opposite: Yoshiaki Izawa played in the 1971 match and earned fourteen caps for his country. He is shown here as he tackles Wales's Phil Bennett in 1973. By then the rugby world was wise to Japan's potential.

A Refreshing Success

First Hong Kong Sevens

1976 The basic idea for a rugby tournament in Hong Kong, one that later turned into a glorious annual event, was aired in a conversation between the chairman of the Hong Kong RFU, a South African entrepreneur called A.D.C. 'Tokkie' Smith, and Ian Gow, a tobacco company executive.

Gow wanted Hong Kong to stage something loosely along the lines of a rugby World cup, though nothing quite as grand as that competition eventually became. Top teams would be invited to play fifteen-a-side matches in whatever format was deemed the most practical. Smith had the foresight to understand that a Sevens Tournament was a more realistic proposition, allowing more matches to be played in one location over a shorter period of time.

With a typically conservative mind-set, the RFU at Twickenham turned down the initial proposal. That left the HKRFU with the more limited plan of inviting countries from Asia and the Pacific. The first tournament at Happy Valley in March 1976 attracted national sides from Korea, Tonga, Japan, Sri Lanka, Malaysia and Fiji. Australia and New Zealand were also invited, but chose to send club teams as representatives. When both those sides, the Wallaroos from Australia and the Christchurch-based Cantabrians from New Zealand, reached the final, that looked like a sensible decision. The Cantabrians triumphed 24-8 in front of three thousand supporters.

The tournament was such a refreshing success that it was destined to grow in stature. The Hong Kong Sevens were born.

Opposite: Fans still flock to watch the games at the Hong Kong Sevens.

Toshiyuki Hayashi

Representing the Best of Rugby

1980s Toshiyuki Hayashi could be described as the first Japanese rugby legend. The brilliant lock, who sharpened his game playing in one of Oxford University's most successful teams, won thirty-eight caps for Japan. He captained his country in 1987, and when they enjoyed any kind of glorious moment in their international history, you could bet that Hayashi was there, playing a central role in the upset.

So it was when Japan beat Scotland in Tokyo in 1989, when a rampant Hayashi even scored one of the home side's tries. He celebrated the following year with a storming performance for Oxford in their Varsity Match victory against Cambridge. When the Japanese overran Zimbabwe in Belfast at the 1991 World Cup, Hayashi was right in the thick of the action, still going strong and inspiring his pack to greater things.

In his native Japan, he slowly grew famous, even though soccer is their bigger sport. Hayashi's rugby club was Kobe Steel and he played an important part in its pre-eminence in Japanese domestic rugby, while trying to ensure that competition in his country was healthily strong across the board. Hayashi and his headband represented the best of Japanese rugby through the 1980s and beyond.

Toshiyuki Hayashi (pictured moving in to tackle Cambridge in 1990)

Born: 8 February 1960

Place of birth: Tokushima, Japan

Caps: 21

Teams: Oxford University, Japan

Aussies Thrill at Hong Kong

Just Reward for Supporting Hong Kong Sevens

1980s Not many rugby minnows can claim to have taken on New Zealand and won, but Hong Kong did in 1982–83. The tension dated back to 1977, the second year of the tournament, when Australia realized the Hong Kong Sevens were ready for take-off and sent a national team. The problem was that New Zealand refused to show the same respect, sending Marlborough instead. The situation came to a head in 1982, when Hong Kong decided not to invite New Zealand unless they were prepared to send a side under the national banner. They were not, so the tournament kicked off without a New Zealand representative for the only year in its history.

Australia, meanwhile, received their just reward for having supported the Hong Kong Sevens at all times and produced some scintillating rugby that year to take the title. By 1983 New Zealand had realized the error of its ways and sent its national side to Hong Kong at last. It did not make any difference, because David Campese had arrived on what was to become one of his favourite stages.

In 1983 he combined with Mark and Glen Ella to give one of the most spectacular and joyous demonstrations of running rugby the world has ever seen. They retained the title, beating Fiji in the final, then 'Campo' and Mark Ella translated their newfound partnership on to the fifteens stage for a devastating Wallabies tour of the UK the following year.

Australia won Hong Kong again in 1985 and 1988, Campese winning Player of the Tournament at the latter festival. Australia was always good to Hong Kong and, during the 1980s in particular, Hong Kong repaid Australia with interest.

Opposite: David Campese – Australia's star of the Hong Kong Sevens.

Arguably Japan's Finest Hour

Japan 28 Scotland 24

1989 The 'Cherry Blossoms' ran in 5 tries against a strong and overconfident Scotland side that never quite recovered from a first-half hammering in Tokyo. The tourists refused to use a kicking tee and missed 7 penalties between them, although scrum-half Greig Oliver did manage to notch up 17 points without any help. Since the Scots were already 20-6 down by the break, Oliver had little choice if his team were to stay in the game at all. Jim Hay, the hooker, burst through for his country's only try; otherwise the Japanese tackled hard when they could and gave away penalties when they could not.

Scotland did not award caps and were missing nine British Lions, who were on tour in Australia at the time; but that should not detract from Japan's achievement. The Cherry Blossoms' legendary lock, Toshiyuki Hayashi, still had Damien Cronin to jump against at line-outs, and scored a try nevertheless. Sean Lineen was still a formidable presence in Scotland's centre, but could not stop Japan's Eiji Kutsuki from cutting through to touch down as well.

The wingers, Yoshida and Nohumuri, both went over, while from full-back the surprisingly prolific Yamamoto scored a try, kicked a conversion and slotted 2 penalties for good measure.

By the time it was all over, Japan's captain, Seiji Hirao, had reason to feel proud. From fly-half, he had unleashed his three-quarters at the right time and inspired his men when the going got tough. For the Scotland XV it was a long journey home, knowing they had just entered rugby history for all the wrong reasons.

Opposite: Seiji Hirao, captain of the proud Japanese team of 1989, who went on to become coach.

Hong Kong Sevens' Heroes

Glorious Fiji

1990–92 The words Hong Kong and Fiji, when put together, conjure magical memories in the minds of all rugby fans. As the Hong Kong Sevens continued to expand, with growing numbers of participants and crowds, so the quality of rugby seemed also to rise.

It was Fiji who took the art of Sevens to a new level in 1990. Waisale Serevi had already won Player of the Tournament in 1989, though New Zealand had triumphed in the tournament. Now the two giants of the Sevens game, Fiji and New Zealand, were doing battle for the title, and the New Zealanders were 10-6 ahead.

Then came the sequence of events since described as the most mesmerizing piece of rugby ever seen. Trapped in their own half, Fiji began to improvise. Vesito Raulumi launched a one-handed missile to Serevi, who tapped it volleyball style over his head to Noa Nadruku before he could be tackled. With New Zealand pressing as one, Noa Nadruku slipped the ball through his legs to evade Terry Wright.

Finally, through a combination of passes of which the Harlem Globetrotters would have been proud, the move had reached Tomasi Cama, the bearded winger. The explosive pace seemed to come from nowhere as he skipped past the legendary John Gallagher, almost as if mocking him, and left the entire New Zealand defence for dead to score under the posts. Fiji in top gear are unstoppable, and a six-feet-seven-inch-tall forward called Mesake Rasrari secured the crown with two more tries.

The captaincy passed from Alifereti Dere to Sami Rabaka between 1990 and 1992, but Ratu Kitione Vesiluka remained coach and Fiji stayed unbeaten. If there is one reason why the Hong Kong Sevens are so adored, it is because of the fabulous Fijians.

Opposite: Waisale Serevi in his element at the Hong Kong Sevens in 1993.

Rugby World Cup

Japan 52 Zimbabwe 8

1991 It does not get much better than running in 9 tries at a Rugby World Cup, and Japan discovered such a thrill at the 1991 tournament just before it was too late. Hard as the Cherry Blossoms fought, a 47-9 defeat to Scotland at Murrayfield had not been the ideal way to introduce themselves to British fans. They were unfortunate enough to face a second match on their opposition's home turf when they took on Ireland in Dublin a few days later. Under the circumstances, Japan's defeat by 32-16 was perfectly respectable. However, there was one more chance to go out in a blaze of glory when they played Zimbabwe at Ravenhill, Belfast.

The Africans must have been thinking along the same lines and put up some decent resistance in the first half to limit the score to 16-4. When the Japanese cut loose after the break, they played some of the finest rugby that has ever been seen from an Asian international team. Terunori Masuho was only nineteen and had a dream afternoon on the wing, scoring 2 tries. He was not alone. Yoshihito Yoshida ran in another 2 on the other wing, and Eiji Kutsuki did the same down the centre. Of the 9 tries that he attempted to convert, Takahiro Hosokawa managed 5, adding 2 more penalties to bring his personal tally to 16.

It was Japan's sweetest World Cup moment, and one to savour as they went home. Going into the 2007 tournament, it remains their only World Cup victory.

Opposite: Yoshihito Yoshida, one of Japan's World Cup scorers.

A Golden Era

Unstoppable All Blacks Take Hong Kong Sevens

1994–96 First the Hong Kong Sevens was staged at the Football Club's stadium in Happy Valley. Then, in 1982, to cope with the added interest, the tournament moved to the Hong Kong Government Stadium. When that ground was not large enough to keep pace with the way rugby's 'Jewel in the Crown' was growing by 1994, it was decided to build an even bigger arena, the magnificent 40,000 Hong Kong Stadium.

The new venue needed a big act to match its impressive capacity – and it got just that. The years from 1994 to 1996 were the golden era of the unbeatable rugby giants of New Zealand. The immense talents of Jonah Lomu and Christian Cullen first found a huge, appreciative stage in Hong Kong. No one had ever seen anyone quite like Lomu before, and the Hong Kong Sevens gave the man-mountain a chance to hone his handling skills as well as display his incredible power and pace.

New Zealand won in 1994 and 1995, by which time Cullen had also erupted on to the Hong Kong scene and found the perfect place to showcase his own unique talents. In many ways he was at the opposite end of the physical scale to Lomu, especially at that early stage of his career. Cullen's blistering pace, coupled with a lovely side-step, made him even more unplayable in Hong Kong than the mighty Jonah had been.

In 1996, Cullen's explosive talent reached an early peak and he simply ran riot at the tournament. With 18 tries, 7 in a single match, the dynamic youngster was poetry in motion as he powered past opponents and smashed all records. Twenty-two conversions took his points tally to 136. He was rugby's new sensation.

Opposite: The triumphant New Zealand captain Eric Rush (left) and Christian Cullen hoist the Hong Kong Sevens trophy in 1996.

Record Defeat at Rugby World Cup

Japan 17 New Zealand 145

1995 Score two tries against the All Blacks in a World Cup match and you are normally close to rugby deification. The problem for Japan's defiant flanker, Hiroyuki Kajihara, was that New Zealand scored 21 tries in the same game, which slightly overshadowed Kajihara's impressive achievement. It might not have been quite so bad (though that is hard to imagine) had Japan been playing New Zealand's strongest team, but this was virtually a second-string fifteen, while the real stars were taking a rest before greater challenges.

Simon Culhane alone scored 45 points, notching a try and 20 conversions. Yes, he missed one, though his consolation was the World Cup record for individual points in a match. Marc Ellis ran in 6 tries (also the most in any World Cup match so far) and he scored another elsewhere in the tournament to put him equal second for individual tries in any World Cup, just behind the great Jonah Lomu, who got 8 that year.

Japan's record defeat was the most points any international team had conceded at the time, and by the biggest margin too. Suddenly, that glorious day in Belfast four years earlier seemed a lifetime away. Japan shares with the USA a particular affection for winners rather than losers, so rugby's popularity took a heavy blow that day. It did not take the rugby men in Tokyo long to work out that the only way to lay the ghost of a record defeat was to beat someone else by even more, though such a victory would be a good few years in the making.

Opposite: Japanese coach Osamu Koyabu, confident on 27 May 1995. Japan was to go on to lose against Wales and Ireland before the crushing match against New Zealand.

Andrew McCormick

The First 'Foreign' Captain of Japan

1990s Andrew McCormick started out wanting to follow in the footsteps of his father, Fergie McCormick, and become an All Black. In many ways, he ended up doing something even more extraordinary. Nicknamed Angus, the younger McCormick came close to achieving his original ambition. While playing for Canterbury in New Zealand, the powerful centre became an All Black trialist. The problem was that he did not make it into the New Zealand side and, for one reason or another, did not feel he would ever be given the chance. Rather than stick around and be 'the rugby player who did not get quite as far as his father' for the rest of his life, he realized it was time to look for new horizons.

In 1992, he accepted an offer to play for Toshiba Fuchu in Japan. He was set apart from a few other Japanese imports because he immersed himself in the local culture and learned fluent Japanese to become extremely popular with his team-mates. He became captain in 1994 and did the job for four seasons, leading his side to one title after another.

By 1996 he had qualified to play for Japan in the Pacific Rim Championship, and never looked back. He played twenty-five times for his adopted country, and had the honour of becoming Japan's first 'foreign' captain, even leading them in the 1999 World Cup. Results did not go according to plan and Japan suffered three quite heavy defeats, though nothing on the scale of the defeat to McCormick's mother country at the previous World Cup. In many ways he had steadied the ship, however, and he always served Japan with honour. He was an All Black's son who ended up in the Land of the Rising Sun.

Andrew McCormick

Born: 5 February 1967
Place of birth: New Zealand
Caps: 23
Teams: Toshiba Fuchu, Japan

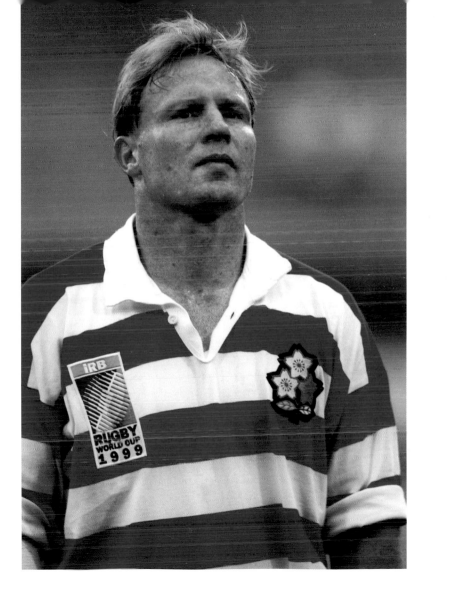

Lebanon Beat France 36-6

First Ever Rugby League International in Middle East

2002 Lebanon may seem the unlikeliest place for a rugby league success story, but not when you consider how many Lebanese live in inner-city Sydney, Australia. The Cedars, as the national team is known, started out packed with Australian-born stars to inspire the rise of the game, such that there is now a healthy league in Lebanon. If the Cedars keep winning (as was their habit between 2002 and 2006), more and more Lebanon-born players will break through to maintain a phenomenon that is Asian, even though the regular opposition seems to be European or African.

Lebanon's 36-6 win over France in 2002, with John Elias (who founded Lebanese Rugby League in 1995) as coach, was a catalyst for an impressive four-year run of results. Robbie Farah scored the opening try, along with tries by Samer al Masri (captain for the game, and known as 'al Magic' in Australia) and Frank Samia.

By 2006, both coach and star forward, Robbie Farah of Wests Tigers, had helped to earn a new depth of respect for the nation's work in the game. Farah is rated so highly as hooker that Australia could soon steal him and, with that in mind, his contribution to Lebanon's international adventure is already becoming problematic.

Lebanon won the Mediterranean Cup in 2003 with a 102-0 demolition of Serbia, a 60-0 drubbing of Morocco and another win against France, this time 26-18. The following year they repeated the feat, with Serbia again the biggest victims at the wrong end of a 64-6 thrashing; Morocco were dispatched 48-14; and France 42-12, a huge win over a once-proud rugby league nation. The Phoenician Cup followed in 2006, with victory over Malta by 36-10. On 28 October of the same year Lebanon beat Russia 28-8 in a World Cup qualifier. From a country too often associated with war and misery, this is an impressive story of growth against the odds.

Opposite: Lebanon's Hazem El-Masri in action; he scored six goals against France in 2002.

Japan Show No Mercy to Taiwan

Japan 155 Taiwan 3

2002 Knowing what it was like to be on the receiving end of a world-record defeat did not tempt Japan to show mercy on Taiwan in 2002 – quite the reverse. As far as possible, the Japanese wanted their own name wiped from that particular section of the record books and they launched into their opposition with considerable ruthlessness. There were 8 tries for Daisuke Ohata alone, meaning he had already reached a landmark 30 in his test career. Meanwhile, Japan-born Andrew Miller kept the scoreboard ticking with 12 conversions, even though he was not given kicking responsibilities for more than half the match. Toru Kurihara was the other marksman, and he added a try to his own tally of 12 conversions. There were 23 tries in all, and poor Taiwan could not even claim they had tired in the second half, because they were 71-3 behind at half-time.

Japan had put 134 points on the minnows in Taipei at the Asian Championships in 1998 and no one thought they would score more. Now that they had, it was not New Zealand who held the record for the most points ever scored in a test match (for their massacre of Japan at the 1995 World Cup) but the Japanese themselves who could claim the title, as well as the biggest ever margin of victory.

At the same time, however, they had to be careful about where such results might lead. As the strongest Asian nation, Japan needed more resilient local opposition in order to prepare themselves adequately for World Cup matches. It was in their interest to ensure that the game continued to thrive in the region and huge defeats over their rivals did not necessarily help. On this occasion though, Japan could be forgiven their relief – delight even – at having moved on from the nightmare of New Zealand in South Africa.

Opposite: The Japanese team in 2001, including Toru Kurihara – most would go on to crush Taiwan in 2002.

England Rule In Hong Kong

Thrilling Team on a Roll

2002–04 England did not have too many superstars at the Hong Kong Sevens between 2002 and 2004, but they had a thrilling team that could not stop winning. In 2003, they also had a very poignant motivating force behind them. Looking back, Josh Lewsey's involvement in the first triumph in 2002 was England's answer to the introduction of superstars from other countries in previous years. Lewsey went on to win the World Cup the following year and scored the deciding try against Wales in the Hong Kong semi-final in 2002.

The star of the show was James Simpson-Daniel, whose blistering hat-trick put paid to the Fijians in the final. Further scores from a Cambridge student, Simon Amor, and Ben Gollings, a Cornishman, made for an impressive 30-20 win over the most famous rugby sevens nation on the planet.

The England success of 2003 was perhaps the hardest to achieve both physically and emotionally. Nick Duncombe, also a Sevens star for his country, had died in the previous month at the age of twenty-one. 'We spoke about absent friends,' revealed the England coach, Joe Lydon, describing mental preparations for the latter stages of the competition. It seemed to fire England, who could not have had it any harder. They had to beat Australia in the quarter-final, Fiji in the semi-final, and New Zealand in the showpiece itself.

Henry Paul was outstanding, but Richard Haughton stole the headlines, coming on as a replacement to show his pace as a Saracens winger by dashing in for 2 tries in three minutes. England had beaten the best and won the final 22-17. By the time the 2004 final came around, Amor was calling the shots and he scored his side's first try against Argentina. Haughton burst through for his own touchdown and Rob Thirlby settled it with a final try for a 22-12 victory. Three titles in a row was some achievement. Duncombe would have been proud of his mates.

Opposite: England's Henry Paul (centre) breaks through the Fiji defence in the Hong Kong Sevens, March 2002. England won the match 19-12.

Super Powers Cup

Japan Beat Russia and Canada

2004 One way to ensure they were still competitive against better-prepared teams than Taiwan was for Japan to compete in the Super Powers Cup. They hosted the second tournament in Tokyo in 2004 and were determined to win in style.

Japan beat Russia 29-12 in their first match, with their scrum-half, Wataru Ikeda, running the show. Not only did he score a try but Ikeda also added 2 conversions and 5 penalties to bring his personal haul to 24 points. Takafumi Hirao, the winger, supplied the other try, and the Japanese were one step from achieving their objective.

Victory against Canada would clinch the title, but their hopes looked doomed when they fell 18-10 behind by half-time. Desperate not to lose in front of their own crowd, the Cherry Blossoms poured through the Canadian lines to rattle up a thrilling 34-21 win. There were tries for Daisuke Ohata and Kjohei Morita, who also kicked a penalty. Even the captain and number eight, Takuro Miuchi, seized a chance to dive over, and a utility back called Koichi Ohigashi completed the fireworks. This time Ikeda had kicked all 4 conversions and a penalty, taking his tally for the two matches to 35.

USA and Russia were reduced to playing each other in the third place play-off match, with the Americans taking the consolation prize. Japan were not a rugby super power, but they had won the Super Powers Cup, and it was one of their finest hours.

Opposite: Japan's Hitoshi Oono jumps highest to claim the ball at a line-out in the 29-12 game against Russia on 27 May 2004.

Charity Match

Rugby Unites to Help Asia After Tsunami

2005 When the Tsunami swept through Asia on Boxing Day 2004, Sri Lankan rugby players and their families were among its victims. Ruhunu RFU, for example, reported four players killed, the relatives of many others swept away, the homes of countless more destroyed. An insignificant detail, given the scale of the tragedy, was that rugby grounds in Koggala, St Aloysius and Matara had their facilities washed away.

It was not the damage to Asian rugby that prompted top players to participate in a match between the Northern and Southern Hemispheres, organized early the following year and played on 5 March 2005, but the stories of human suffering that were simply too numerous to recount. Rugby people wanted to help survivors get back on their feet as best they could. Lawrence Dallaglio, who knew the pain of losing a loved one to drowning, said before the Rugby Aid match at Twickenham, 'I think we are all deeply affected by the Tsunami disaster and this match gives rugby and us as players a unique opportunity to do something very special, to raise a lot of money for an incredibly worthwhile cause.'

Eleven tries were scored as South beat North 54-19 and Man of the Match, Chris Latham, said after scoring 2 tries, 'This was one of the best games of rugby I've ever been involved in.' The money raised was staggering. The International Rugby Board (IRB) was able to hand over 3,349,943 US Dollars to the World Food Programme, the largest single donation ever received from an individual sporting event. 'Rugby can be proud of this result,' said Syd Millar, the IRB Chairman. The money did not bring anyone back but it might have made a few lives more bearable, even in the Sri Lankan rugby community of Ruhunu.

Opposite: Princes William (right) and Harry applaud the teams during the benefit match at Twickenham.

LANDMARK

Asia's Trail-Blazing Success

Daisuke Ohata Breaks Campo's Try-Scoring Record

2006 On May 14, 2006, Daisuke Ohata ran in 3 tries for Japan against Georgia's Lelos in a 32-7 victory at the Hanazono Stadium in his native Osaka. In doing so, he broke the international try-scoring record set by David Campese of Australia. It would be stretching the achievement to claim that Ohata is the greatest international try-scorer of all time; but he is certainly the most prolific that rugby union has seen so far.

'Campo' amassed 64 touch-downs the hard way, often against the best sides in the world, and it took him 101 tests to do it. For Ohata, the task was sometimes more routine, such as for the 8 tries he managed in Japan's 155-point demolition of Taiwan four years earlier. However, that should not detract from the Japanese heart-throb's ruthless efficiency, because he took only 55 games to set the new world record of 65.

It has been a strange roller-coaster ride for Ohata. Either Japan matches were so easy that the winger was scoring for fun or they were so tough that he was unable to make an impression. Such extremes tend to even out over a player's career, despite the dubious quality of much of Japan's opposition. No one would argue that Ohata is a better player than Campese, but the new record can only be good for rugby union.

Asia has a new champion, a symbol of the continent's relentless quest to receive recognition and respect in the rugby world. When Japan hosts the Rugby World Cup, as sooner or later the country is sure to do, that will bring a further huge boost to the development of the game. For now, Ohata is blazing the trail; the rest of Asia's turn for rugby greatness may not be far away.

Opposite: Daisuke Ohata is tackled by Arabian Gulf's Dushan Raveendrakumar (left) and James Tometzki during the Asian qualifying match for the 2007 World Cup. Japan stormed ahead and won the game 82-9.

Index

Page numbers in *italics* refer to picture captions

Ackford, Paul 324
Afeaki, Inoke 284
al Masri, Samer 368
All Blacks 18, 126 *see also* New Zealand
Amor, Simon 372
Andes air crash 308
Andrew, Rob 202
Argentina
  history (union) 302, 306, 312–15
  internationals (league) 336
  internationals (union) 306, 312, 314, 324, 328, 334, 338
  tours (union) 306
  World Cup (union) 76, 92, 314, 330
Ashworth, John 184
Asian Championships 370
Australia
  Ashes (league)
    1940s 146
    1950s 154, 160, 166
    1960s 46, 48
    1970s 170, 270
    1980s 64, 66, 198
    1990s 90, 198
    2000s 118
  Grand Slams 68
  history (league) 20, 160
  history (union) 266, 268
  Hong Kong Sevens 348, 352, 372
  internationals (league) 36, 46, 48, 66, 264, 332

internationals (union)
  Argentina 312, 314
  British Lions 112
  England 44, *56*, 68, 150, 202
  Fiji 44
  Ireland 68
  New Zealand 28, 50, 52, 68, 104
  Scotland 68
  South Africa 34, 44, 252, 254, 260, 266, 268
  Tonga 56
  Wales 44, 68
  tours (union) 34, 68
  Tri-Nations (league) 32, 122, 124, 238
  Tri-Nations (union) 96, 104
  World Cup (league) 36, 48, 90, 118, 120, 178, 240, 258, 282
  World Cup (union)
    1991 (winners) *56*, 78, 80, 82, 84, 86, 88, 92, 224
    1999 (winners) 84, 102, 104, 296
    2003 106, 226, 228, 230
Australian Police Rugby League 336

Bachop, Stephen 92
Balshaw, Iain 338
Barbarians 40, 54, 58, 162, 164, 180
Barends, David 270
Barnard, Johan *278*
Barry, Joe 246

Batibasaga, Asaeli 54
Baxter, Tom 32
Beaumont, Bill 58, 140, 190
Benazzi, Abdel 280
Bennett, Phil 54, 58, 180, *346*
Bennett, Wayne *90,* 122, 332
Bernat-Salles, Philippe 216
Berrigan, Shaun 332
Bevan, Brian 152, 206
Blanco, Serge 188, 196
Bledisloe Cup 28, 106
Bloomfield, Tevita 70
Bolton, David 160
Boston, Billy 152, 156, 256
Botha, Naas 272, 284, 296
Bowen, Bleddyn 70
Bowen, Matt 332
British and Irish Lions (2001 onwards) 112, 234, 334
British Asian Rugby Association (BARA) 360
British Lions (up to 2001)
  vs. Australia 112
  vs. Fiji 58
  vs. New Zealand 74, 116, 164, 172, 208
  vs. South Africa 182, 186, 190, 214, 260, 272
  see also British and Irish Lions
Brito, Max 284
Brown, 'Bruno' 138
Brown, Craig *276*
Brown, Dave 262
Brown, Mark 70
Brown, 'Spanner' 34
Bruce, Doug 60
Buchanan, Angus *134*
Bunce, Frank 92

Burcher, David
Burke, Cyril 34
Burke, Matthew 104, 112
Burlington, Ed 316
Butt, Ikram 360

Cakobau, Ratu Sir George 30
Cama, Tomasi 356
Camberabero, Guy and Lilian 168
Campaes, André 168
Campese, David ('Campo') 68, 78, 84, 88, 352, 378
Canada 300, 316, 318, 320, 322, 326, 344, 374
Canessa, Roberto 308
Carling, Will 88, 94, 200, 202, 232
Carlson, Brian 36
Carney, Brian 238
Carrere, Christian 168
Carroll, Daniel 304
Carter, Dan 110, 128
Catchpole, Ken 44
Catt, Mike 94
Cavubati, Bill *30*
Celaya, Michel 158
Challenge Cup (league) 146, 152, *160*, 166, 178, 206, 240, 256
Challinor, Jim 160
Charron, Al 320, 326
Chichibu, Prince 344
Cilley, José 328
Clarke, Don ('The Boot') 38
Clarke, Edward Bramwell 342
Clarkson, Joe *316*
Cleaveland, Norman 304
Coates, Vincent 138

Conteponi, Felipe 338
Cooper, Matt 332
Corleto, Ignacio 330
Cornelsen, Greg 52
Costin, Brandon 332
Craven, Danie 252, 258
Cronin, Damien 354
Cross, William *134*
Crowley, Dan 102
Culhane, Simon 364
Cullen, Christian 110, 362

Dacey, Malcolm 70
Dallaglio, Lawrence 226, 376
Daly, Jack 148
David, Tom 180
Davies, Adrian 326
Davies, Alan 326
Davies, Dave 138
Davies, Gerald 172
Davies, Jonathan 70, 194
Davies, Phil 70
Dawes, John 172, 180
Dawson, Matt 214, 226
De Carli, Giampiero 218
de C.M. Heriot, F. 302
Dere, Alifereti 356
Devereux, John 90
Doe, Charles 304
Dominguez, Diego ('The Little
    Magician') 218, 220
Dominici, Christian 216
Douga, Benoit 168
Dourthe, Richard 216
du Plessis, Morne 268
du Preez, Frik 260
du Toit, Pier 40
Dubai Sevens *246*
Duckham, David 54, 164
Duncombe, Nick 372
Duprat, Bernard 168
Dwyer, Bob 108

Eales, John ('Nobody') 102,

104, 106, 112
Eastlake, Cyril 32
Edwards, Gareth 54, 172,
    176, 180, 292
El-Masri, Hazem 368
Elias, John 368
Ella, Mark 68, 352
Ella brothers 66, 68, 352
Ellis, Marc 364
England
    Five Nations (union) 138,
        148, 168, 190, 200,
        202, 208
    Grand Slams 138, 140, 150,
        202, 224
    history (union) 132, 134,
        138–41, 144, 150, 302
    Hong Kong Sevens 372
    internationals (union)
        Argentina 302, 312, 338
        Australia 44, 56, 68, 150,
            202
        France 150
        Japan 346
        New Zealand 60, 116, 144
        Scotland 26, 134, 150
        South Africa 248, 254,
            260, 274
    rugby league *see* Great
        Britain
    Six Nations (union) 236
    Triple Crown (union) 150
    World Cup (union)
        1991 *56*, 78, 82, 86, 88,
            224
        1995 92, 94, 228
        1999 232
        2003 (winners) 106, 222,
            224, 226, 228, 230
España, Eduardo 306
Evans, Eric 150
Evans, Stuart 70

Farah, Robbie 368

Farr-Jones, Nick 82, 88
Fernandez, Nicolas *334*
Fiji
    the Cibi 30
    Hong Kong Sevens 108,
        356, 372
    internationals (union) 24, 30,
        44, 54, 58, 70, 116
    Pacific Rim Championship
        (union) 114
    tours (union) 30, 54
    World Cup (league) 282
    World Cup (union) 74, 76, 320
Fitzpatrick, Sean 94, 96
Five Nations *see under*
    individual countries
Flatley, Elton 226
Flood, Toby 338
Fox, Grant 38, 74, 76, 100,
    110, 128
France
    Five Nations (union) 138,
        148, 158, 168, 202,
        208, 210
    Grand Slams 168, 280
    history (league) 142
    history (union) 158, 168, 304
    internationals (league) 36, 48,
        166, 178, 258, 294, 368
    internationals (union) 150,
        192, 248, 254, 260,
        268, 312
    Olympic Games 304
    Six Nations (union) 234, 236
    tours (union) 98, 268
    World Cup (league) 36, 48,
        154, 258
    World Cup (union)
        1987 72, 74, 76, 276
        1991 320
        1995 280
        1999 102, 104, 216
        2003 226
Francis, Nell *276*

Fraser, Eric 160
Fraser, W.L. 302

Gachassin, Jean 168
Galia, Jean 142
Gallagher, John 356
Gallaher, Dave 18
Galthié, Fabien 216
Gasnier, Reg ('Puff the Magic
    Dragon') 46
Gear, Rico 116
Gebbie, Oswald 302
Georgia 242, 378
Gibbs, Scott 214
Gibson, Mike 174
Golden Boot award (rugby
    league) 118, 120, 124, 198
Gollings, Ben 372
Gourdon, Jean-François 184
Gow, Ian 348
Grau, Roberto 330
Great Britain/England (league)
    Ashes
        1940s 146
        1950s 154, 160, 166
        1960s 46, 48
        1970s 170, 270
        1980s 64, 66, 198
        1990s 90, 198, 282
        2000s 118
    history 136, 146, 160
    internationals 156, 166,
        178, 262
    tours 146
    Tri-Nations 122, 238, 240
    World Cup 36, 48, 90, 120,
        178, 240, 258
Greenwood, Col 264
Gregan, George 106
Gregan, Sean 224
Griffiths, Fred 264
Grigg, Peter 68
Guest, Dicky 148
Guscott, Jeremy 88, 202, 214

Hadden, Frank 116
Haden, Andy 60
Hadley, Adrian 70
Haig, Jim 32
Hanley, Ellery ('The Black
    Pearl', 'Mr Magic') 198
Harris, Mark *170*
Harrison, Justin 112
Hart, John 80, 216
Hastings, Gavin 208, 210
Haughton, Richard 372
Hawthorne, Phil 44
Hay, Jim 354
Hayashi, Toshiyuki 350, 354
Hayden, Andy *62*
Hayes, John *330*
Heatlie, Barry 246
Henry, Graham *28,* 112, 116
Henson, Gavin 236
Herbert, Daniel 112
Hewson, Alan 62
Hiller, Bob 168
Hirao, Seiji 354
Hirao, Takafumi 374
Hong Kong Sevens 348, 352,
    362 *see also under*
    individual countries
Horan, Tim 84, 88, 102
Horne, Willie 154
Hosokawa, Takahiro 358
Hughes, Mac 34

Ikeda, Wataru 374
Ireland
    Five Nations (union) 138,
        148, 168
    Grand Slams 148
    history (union) 148
    internationals (union) 60, 68,
        116, 248, 254, 278
    Six Nations (union) 234, 236
    Triple Crown (union) 234
    World Cup (union) 82, 102,
        276, 330, 358

Irvine, Andy 188, 190
Italy 72, 76, 80, 218, 220,
    236, 278
Ivory Coast 284
Izawa, Yoshiaki *346*

Jaguars 310
James, Billy 70
James, Carwyn 164, 172
Japan
    history (union) 342–47
    internationals (union) 344,
        346, 350, 354, 370,
        374, 378
    World Cup (union) 276, 316,
        350, 358, 364, 366, *378*
Jenkins, Gareth 236
Jenkins, Neil 326
Jimsheladze, Paliko 242
John, Barry ('The King') 172,
    176
Johns, Andrew ('Joey') 118, 120
Johnson, Martin 112, 214,
    226, 228, 284
Johnstone, Brad 218
Joiner, Craig *284*
Joint, Chris *282*
Jones, Lewis 170
Jones, Michael ('The Iceman')
    80, 114
Jones, Robert 70
Jones, Stacey ('The Little
    General') 120, 122
Joubert, André 292
Joubert, Steve 248

Kajihara, Hiroyuki 364
Kangaroos (league) *see*
    Australia
Karalius, Vince ('Wild Bull') 160
Kearns, Phil 102
Kelly, Ben 332
Kelly, Malcolm 174
Kennedy, Ben 332

Kenny, Brett 64
Kirk, David *76*
Kirkpatrick, Ian 50
Kirksey, Morris 304
Kirwan, John 72, 76
Klaassen, Wynand 62
Knight, Gary 62
Koyabu, Osamu *364*
Krige, 'Japie' 248
Krilich, Max 64
Kuinikoro, Joape 58
Kurihara, Toru 370
Kutsuki, Eiji 354, 358
Kyle, Jackie 148

Lacaze, Claude 168
Lam, Pat 92
Lamaison, Christophe ('Titou')
    98, 216
Lambert, Gary 316
Langlands, Graeme 46
Large, Ken 256
Latham, Chris 376
Latu, Sami 56
Lebanon 368
Leonard, Jason ('The Fun Bus')
    106, 204, 224
Lewis, Wally ('King Wally') 64, 66
Lewsey, Josh 372
Lineen, Sean 354
Little, Jason 102
Little, Nicky 114
Lockyer, Darren 118, 124, 332
Lomu, Jonah 94, 98, 216,
    228, 292, 362, 364
Loubser, 'Bob' 248
Lowe, Cyril 138
Loyola, Raul 306
Luyt, Louis 96
Lydon, Joe 372
Lynagh, Michael 82, 88

MacKinnon, 'Gord' 320
Macqueen, Rod 112

Magne, Olivier 216
Mains, Laurie 286
Malta 368
Mandela, Nelson 280,
    286, 288
Mans, Gerhard 278
Mason, Willie 124, 332
Masuho, Terunori 358
McBride, Willie John 182,
    184, 186
McCaffery, Ken 36
McCaw, Richie 126
McCormick, Andrew
    ('Angus') 366
McCormick, Fergie 176, 366
McGeechan, Ian 60, 214
McKechnie, Brian 60
McKinney, Tom 238
McLennon, Brian 122
McLoughlin, Ian ('Mighty
    Mouse') 172
Meads, Colin ('Pinetree') 42,
    44, 172
Mealamu, Keven 234
Mehrtens, Andrew 100, 104,
    110, 128
Mendez, Federico ('Freddie')
    324
Meninga, Mal 64, 90
Menzies, George 32
Messenger, 'Dally' 20
Mias, Lucien ('Doctor Pack')
    158
Miller, Andrew 370
Millward, Roger 170, 178
Miuchi, Takuro 374
Monks, H.G. 302
Montgomery, Percy 272, 296
Moody, Lewis *334*
Moon, Richard *212*
Moore, Brian 202
Morgan, Kevin 236
Morita, Kjohei 374
Morkel, 'Boy' 250

Morocco 278, 280, 368
Mourie, Graham 60
Muller, Hennie ('The
    Greyhound') 254
Mullin, Brendan 278
Murariu, Florica 192
Murata, Yoshiro 346
Murphy, Alex 160, 166, 206
Myer, Eden 278
Myler, Frank 170

Nadruku, Noa 356
Namibia 278, 280
Naresia, Vuate 58
Nasave, Senitike 54
Nelson, Gideon 304
Nelson, Ray 316
Nepia, George 22
New South Wales Waratahs 26
New Zealand 20
    Flour-Bomb Test (1981) 62
    Grand Slams 60, 116
    the Haka 22, 126
    history (union) 18, 22, 250
    Hong Kong Sevens 110,
        348, 352, 356, 362, 372
    internationals (league) 36, 46,
        66, 156, 166, 264, 270
    internationals (union)
    Argentina 312, 314
    Australia 28, 50, 52, 68, 104
    Barbarians 164, 180
    British and Irish Lions 334
    British Lions 74, 116, 164,
        172, 208
    England 60, 116, 144
    Fiji 30, 116
    Ireland 60, 116
    Scotland 60, 96, 116
    South Africa 42, 96, 116,
        250, 252, 260, 268, 274
    Wales 18, 60, 116, 126
    tours (union) 18, 22, 40, 42,
        50, 252, 268, 312

Tri-Nations (league) 32, 120,
    122, 124
Tri-Nations (union) 96, 110,
    116
World Cup (league) 36, 90,
    118, 120
World Cup (union)
    1987 (winners) 72, 74,
        76, 80
    1991 80, 84, 320
    1995 94, 96, 228, 286,
        364
    1999 98, 100, 102, 216
    2003 106, 226
Norster, Robert 212
Nunez Piossek, José 328, 334

Obolensky, Prince Alexander
    144
O'Driscoll, Brian 234
O'Driscoll, John 190
Ofahengaue, Viliami ('Willy')
    86, 88
Offiah, Martin ('Chariots') 206
O'Gara, Ronan 330
Ogilvie, Canon George 246
Ohata, Daisuke 370, 374, 378
Ohigashi, Koichi 374
Old Christians Rugby Club,
    Uruguay 308
Oliver, Frank 60
Oliver, Greig 354
Olympic Games (1920s) 304
O'Meley, Mark 332
Oono, Hitoshi 374
O'Reilly, Tony 162
Otona, Aitor 306
Outside, Bob 34
Owen, Michael 236

Papua New Guinea 294
Paraguay 328
Parrado, Fernando 308
Pascual, Marcelo 306

Paul, Henry 372
Peacock, Jamie 240
Petersen, Matt 332
Pichot, Agustin 330, 338
Pienaar, Francois 286, 288
Pillman, 'Cherry' 138
Poggi, Eduardo 306
Poole, Dick 36
Porta, Hugo 220, 310, 312,
    314
Portugal 278
Poulton-Palmer, Ronald 138
Prescott, Alan 156, 160
Preston, Jeff 332
Prinsloo, Jan 256
Probyn, Jeff 324
professionalism issues 20,
    136, 142, 194, 212
Pumas see Argentina
Purcell, Mike 316

Qoro, Jo 54
Quesada, Gonzalo 330
Quinlan, Alan 330
Quinnell, Derek 54, 180
Quinnell, Scott 326

Raaff, 'Klondyke' 248
Rabaka, Sami 356
Racika, Antonio 54, 58
racism issues 22, 62, 156,
    250, 266, 268, 270, 274,
    310
Raper, Johnny 48, 204
Raphael, John E. 302
Rasrari, Mesake 356
Raulumi, Vesito 356
Raveendrakumar, Dushan 378
Ravouvou, Nasivi 54
Rees, Gareth 320, 322, 326
Reid, Alex ('Oupa') 246
Reilly, Mal 170
Renouf, Steve ('The Pearl') 90
Rhinos (league) see South

Africa
Richards, Dean 202, 284
Risman, Gus 146
Robinson, Andy 324
Robinson, Jason ('Mr Twinkle
    Toes,' 'Billy Whizz') 222, 226
Roff, Joe 112
Rogers, Steve 64
Romania 102, 192, 194, 208,
    276, 304, 320
Roos, Paul 248
Rowell, Jack 94
Ruddock, Mike 236
Rugby Football Union (RFU) 136
Rugby Union Player'
    Association 212
Russia 368, 374

Sackey, Paul 338
Sadoumy, Jean-Luc 210
Saint-André, Philippe 202, 210
Samia, Frank 368
Sarramoa, Olivier 98
Saurel, Claude 242
Scotland
    Five Nations (union) 54, 138,
        148, 168, 200, 208, 210
    Grand Slams 200, 208
    history (union) 134
    internationals (union)
        Australia 68
        England 26, 134, 150
        Japan 350, 354
        New Zealand 60, 96, 116
        Romania 192
        South Africa 248, 254, 296
    Six Nations (union) 218,
        220, 236
    World Cup (union) 76, 92,
        208, 276, 358
Secar, Gary 60
Senden, Billy 250
Senillosa, Hernan 328
Serbia 368

383

Serevi, Waisale ('The Magician') 108, 356
Simpson-Daniel, James 372
Six Nations see under individual countries
Skene, Alan 264
Slack, Andrew 68
Smith, A.D.C ('Tokkie') 348
Smith, Dr Doug 172
Smith, Greg 114
Smith, Nate 332
Smith, Ollie 334
Sole, David 200
Soler, Facundo 328
Solomon, John 34
South Africa
  Dubai Sevens 246
  Flour-Bomb Test (1981) 62
  Grand Slams 254
  history (league) 258, 262–65, 270, 294
  history (union) 246–53, 266, 268, 274
  internationals (league) 156, 258, 262, 294
  internationals (union)
    Argentina 306
    Australia 34, 44, 252, 254, 260, 266, 268
    British Lions 182, 186, 190, 214, 260, 272
    England 248, 254, 260, 274
    France 158, 260, 268
    Jaguars 310
    New Zealand 42, 96, 116, 250, 252, 260, 268, 274
    Scotland 248, 254, 296
    Wales 248, 252, 254
  tours (league) 264
  tours (union) 62, 248, 250, 252, 254, 266, 268, 274
  Tri-Nations (union) 100
  World Cup (league) 282, 294

World Cup (union)
  1995 (winners) 92, 96, 268, 286, 288, 290, 322
  1999 102, 104, 296
South American Championship 328
Spencer, Carlos 100, 110
Spencer, John 54
Sporleder, Pedro 328
Springboks see South Africa
Stanger, Tony 200, 208
Stegmann, Anton 248
Stewart, Barry 96
Stewart, Scott 320
Stirling, Peter 64
Stoop, Sam 278
Stortoni, Bernardo 328
Stransky, Joel 286, 290
Stuart, Ian 326
Super League 238, 240
Super Powers Cup 374

Tadayuki, Itoh 346
Taiwan 370, 378
Taufahana, Taunaholo 98
Taumalolo, Siua ('Josh') 98
Telfer, Jim 210
Templeton, Robert 304
Tetsunosuke, Onishi 346
Thirlby, Rob 372
Thomas, Gareth 236
Thompson, Jim 170
Thurston, Jonathan 124
Tikoisuva, Pio Bosco 58
Titley, Mark 70
Tobias, Errol 274
Todeschini, Federico 334, 338
Tometzki, James 378
Tonga 24, 30, 56, 70, 98, 284, 294
Townsend, Gregor 210
Tri-Nations (union and league) see under individual countries

Tsimbo, Richard 276
Tsunami Charity Match (Twickenham, 2005) 376
Tuigamala, Inga 222
Tuisese, Ilaitia 54
Tuquiri, Lote 226
Tynan, Chris 320

Uluinayo, Alfie 114
Umaga, Tana 116, 234
Underwood, Rory ('The Flying Winger') 88, 94, 202, 204
Underwood, Tony 94, 204
Uruguay 308
USA 102, 300, 304, 316, 318, 332, 374

Valentine, Dave 154
van der Westhuizen, Joost 292
van Heerden, Johannes 184
Van Vollenhoven, Tom ('Vol') 256
Vatuvei, Manu 122
Vesiluka, Ratu Kitione 356
Villepreux, Pierre 168
Visei, Josaia 54

Wakefield, Wavell ('Wakers'), Baron Wakefield of Kendal 140
Wakefield Trinity 262, 270
Wales
  Five Nations (union) 54, 58, 138, 148, 168, 190
  Grand Slams 138, 236
  history (union) 138
  Hong Kong Sevens 372
  internationals (union)
    Australia 44, 68
    Canada 322, 326
    Fiji 70
    New Zealand 18, 60, 116, 126
    Romania 192, 194

    South Africa 248, 252, 254
    Western Samoa 70
  Six Nations (union) 236
  tours (union) 70
  Triple Crown (union) 194
  World Cup (league) 178, 294
  World Cup (union) 76, 92, 102, 226
Wallabies see Australia
Wallace, 'Johnny' 26
Walters, Kevin 90
Ward, H.E. 302
Webb Ellis, William 132
Weir, Doddie 96
Western Samoa 70, 92, 114
Wheel, Geoff 60
Wheeler, Peter 60
Whineray, Wilson 40
White, Desmond 32
Wilkinson, Jonny 112, 226, 230, 334
William Webb Ellis trophy 76
Williams, Bryan 92, 180
Williams, Chester 92
Williams, Dickie 156
Williams, J.P.R. 172, 180, 182, 184, 196
Williams, Shane 236
Wilson, Jeff 286
Windon, Col 34
Winterbottom, Peter 212
Woodward, Sir Clive 116, 232, 312
World Cup (union and league) see under individual countries
Wright, Terry 356
Wyatt, Mark 320

Yamaguchi, Ryoji 346
Yoshida, Yoshihito 354, 358

Zimbabwe 276, 278, 350, 358